PURITY & HOLINESS

WORKBOOK

By
Bob Tissot and Alex Rahill

A Biblical
Perspective
On Sexuality
and Relationships

Bair Lake Ministries
12500 Prang Street
Jones, Michigan 49061
www.blbc.com or blbc@voyager.net

Published by Omega House Publishing
Cover design by Mazzocchi Group 877-842-6916

ISBN 0-9672519-3-1
Printed in the United States of America

TABLE OF CONTENTS

INTRODUCTION

A MESSAGE FROM THE AUTHORS

As you begin this study, it is our hope that you will grow greatly in the area of commitment to God and to the application of His standards for your life. In light of that goal, it is important that we emphasize several things from the beginning.

The Word of God.
There are many great books available on the subject of sexuality and relationships. However, none is as great as the Bible. It is the ultimate counseling book! In this text you will find that we constantly refer to and defer to the Word of God, recognizing that God's way is perfect (II Samuel 22:31). In order to help you dig into the study of God's Word for yourself, we have set up Dig Deeper sections at the end of each chapter. These studies will allow you to learn what the Bible says concerning the topics we cover. It is not our goal to give you all the answers, but, instead, to encourage you to see for yourself what the Lord has to say in His Word.

Emotional safety.
We realize that the topic of sexuality and holiness is very personal and private. While we deal with these sensitive issues in this book, we hope that you will feel safe and secure as you study and process the teachings we give. While purity and holiness issues are mainly matters to be handled between you and God, you may feel the desire to experience the healing and freedom of meeting with another Christian to confess sin in your life and to have that person pray for you. If God is leading you in that direction, please seek out wise and trusted Christian counsel through a friend, a youth leader, or a pastor. There are many people around you who would be willing to partner with you in your growth in this area of your spiritual life. You simply need to be willing to ask for their help. Don't be hesitant to do so.

Growth and freedom.
Just the fact that you are reading this book tells us that you are seeking God and His will for your life. With that in mind, we have no doubt that you will experience great growth and freedom through this study. Jesus made it clear that those who know and obey His truth will be set free! The message of purity is one of freedom and blessing. "*Blessed are the pure in heart, for they will see God*" (Matthew 5:8). Pray that God will open your eyes to this great truth as you work through the teachings in this text.

It is _not_ too late.
Some of you who are reading this now have already sacrificed your sexual purity. While there may be regrets about your past decisions, you will learn through this study that God not only forgives, but He also heals. While past sin must be addressed, His desire is that we receive His forgiveness and move on from this day forward as "*more than conquerors through him who loved us*" (Romans 8:37). We will talk more about that later in this study, but we want you to be encouraged that God is ready to forgive and to heal when you turn to Him in confession and repentance.

Growth is a process
Purity and holiness is not an instantaneous condition, but, rather, it is a way of life that begins with a decision to obey God. The teaching that you will receive in this study is not a guarantee of success, but it is to be used as a tool to help you in your journey of purity and holiness. It is our intent to steer you to the Lord and His Word while encouraging you to seek out and listen to those who support you in this matter.

For many of you, parents will be key players in teaching, directing and encouraging you in this adventure. "'*Honor your father and mother'* — *which is the first commandment with a promise*" (Ephesians 6:2) is a powerful word to be obeyed. For those of you who are not blessed with parents who are supportive in this area, God's word encourages you with these words from Philippians 4:19: "*And my God will meet all your needs according to his glorious riches in Christ Jesus.*" You are not alone!

Foundational verses
There are two passages that are central to the theme of this study. While many scriptures address the issues of purity, holiness, sexual behavior, marriage, and other relevant issues, the two scriptures that follow sum these teachings up concisely and accurately. It would be valuable for you to commit them to memory.

1 Thessalonians 4:3-8
"*It is God's will that you should be sanctified: that you should avoid sexual immorality; that each of you should learn to control his own body in a way that is holy and honorable, not in passionate lust like the heathen, who do not know God; and that in this matter no one should wrong his brother or take advantage of him. The Lord will punish men for all such sins, as we have already told you and warned you. For God did not call us to be impure, but to live a holy life. Therefore, he who rejects this instruction does not reject man but God, who gives you his Holy Spirit.*"

II Peter 1:3-4
"*His divine power has given us everything we need for life and godliness through our knowledge of him who called us by his own glory and goodness. Through these he has given us his very great and precious promises, so that through them you may participate in the divine nature and escape the corruption in the world caused by evil desires.*"

Purity & Holiness Goals

We will discuss goal setting in more detail in later chapters of this book, but for now let's set some goals for this study. Whether you are working through this book with a group, at a weekend retreat, or on your own, we hope that by the end of this study, you will ...

1. Know God's will regarding sexuality and relationships.

2. Be able to define purity and holiness.

3. Have answers for the following questions:

    a. How do you control your own body in a holy and honorable way?

    b. What is a sexual sin?

    c. What is sexual morality?

4. Have set personal standards of conduct.

5. Have set three personal goals to help in your pursuit of purity and holiness.

6. Have read I Thessalonians 4:3-8 at least twice a day each day of the study.

7. Have memorized I Thessalonians 4:3-8.

Your Goals

Now, it's your turn to look ahead. List below at least three reasons for your desire to participate in this study.

1.

2.

3.

What do you hope to know by the end of this course?

1.

2.

3.

4.

5.

Be an active learner! That means that you need to read the chapters carefully and you need to prayerfully complete the Dig Deeper sections. If you run into areas that you do not understand or that you wish to discuss with someone, seek out spiritual counsel, as mentioned earlier, from a Christian friend, pastor, youth leader, or counselor. If you need or desire help, just ask!

It is our hope that you will experience a great deal of spiritual growth during this study and that your understanding of God and His standards will take on new dimensions. Take a moment now and pray that God would reveal to you the things that He wants you learn during this time. If you are seeking God in prayer and spending time in His Word, you cannot help but grow. We believe that God will honor and bless your desire to know His will in this important area.

Nine Ways to Stay Pure and Holy

1. Know God's Word.

2. Know God's reasons for purity and holiness.

3. Know God's view of purity and holiness.

4. Know God's way to live a pure and holy life.

5. Know God's power for living the life He desires

6. Find friends who are in agreement with a life of purity and holiness.

7. Find support for your decision to live a pure and holy life.

8. Set your standards.

9. Make your commitment.

Journal Page

Dig Deeper

1. Understanding that vocabulary is important to meaningful discussion, how would you define the following terms?

   Purity

   Holiness

   Dating

   Courting

   Abstinence

   Sexual immorality

2. What is a sexual sin?

3. What does it mean to control one's body in a way that is holy and honorable?

4. What is love?

5. What is lust?

Love

is always about giving.

Lust

is always about taking.

An Attractive House

It was an attractive house. My new wife and I were looking to buy our first home, a place where we could start our family. The house we were touring had a Victorian look with newly painted blue siding and intricate white trim. It was large enough for a couple with an active youth ministry. The lawn was well taken care of and had some beautiful trees on the surrounding property.

There was really only one problem. All the rooms on one side of the house seemed to drop several inches.

"Why do all the floors slant?" my wife asked me in a whisper.

I was her husband, a man, and thought I should know the answer to her question, so I boldly answered, "Uh well it's an old house, and old houses are well…old."

As we finished the tour, we passed one door that we had not yet opened. "What's in there?" I asked.

"Oh nothing, just the basement," said the real estate agent.

As the three of us went downstairs, we found the problem that impacted the three floors above which contained the kitchen, family room, office, and the bedroom. There was a massive crack in the foundation and that crack stretched the entire length of the house. It was positioned in such a way that I could tell that the damage was only going to get worse.

"What are all those water stains along the wall?" I asked.

"The basement must have flooded during that really big storm we had a few weeks ago," the realtor replied. The water stains on the walls stretched two feet above the ground. The problems upstairs suddenly made a lot of sense as it became obvious that this house had trouble, big trouble, with its foundation.

What does this story have to do with life and relationships? A lot. In a house, just like in life, the things that you can't see eventually affect the things that you can.

How can a young man keep his way pure?
This is an important question and relates directly to what we are beginning to study. Just as in the story about the house, the things that you can't see eventually affect the things that you can.

That's why you have to start at the place that matters the most—the foundation. How can a young man keep his way pure? Both the question and its answer are found in Psalm 119:9, *"How can a young man keep his way pure? By living according to your word."*

It's that simple. First, note that there are two factors involved here:

Knowing God's Word, and

Living according to it.

Jesus also very clearly taught that it was not enough to simply know His Word; that knowledge had to be put into practice. He said, *"Why do you call me, 'Lord, Lord,' and do not do what I say? I will show you what he is like who comes to me and hears my words and puts them into practice. He is like a man building a house, who dug down deep and laid the foundation on rock. When the flood came, the torrent struck that house but could not shake it, because it was well built. But the one who hears my words and does not put them into practice is like a man who built a house on the ground without a foundation. The moment the torrent struck that house, it collapsed and its destruction was complete"* (Luke 6:46-49)

I don't know if anyone has warned you, but a flood is coming. Notice Jesus didn't say "if" but "When *the flood came."* Now is your chance to get your foundation set. Maybe for you the flood has already hit. If so, there's still hope. Read on.

Can I ask you a few very important questions? What is the foundation of your life? What is the foundation of your relationships? By that I mean this: What underlies and supports everything you do in your life and your relationships? Whose word are you living by? Yours? Your friends'?

Or, are you living your life and relationships based on God's Word in a relationship with His son, Jesus? *"For no-one can lay any foundation other than the one already laid, which is Jesus Christ"* (I Corinthians 3:11). If you are building your life on anything other than Jesus Christ, you are building on a bad foundation. In fact, just like we showed in the example at the beginning of this chapter, building on a bad foundation will lead to damage in every one of the key "rooms" of your life. The good news is that you can replace that cracked and faulty foundation today.

You may be saying, "I'm a Christian. If Jesus is my Savior, then what do I need to replace? Isn't my foundation already good enough?"

Notice again what Jesus said: *"Why do you call me, 'Lord, Lord,' and do not do what I say? I will show you what he is like who comes to me and hears my words and puts them into practice."* As the Lord teaches us new things, we need to put them into practice. This is what Jesus calls laying a good foundation – not just hearing what He says or believing what He says, but doing what He says. Jesus needs to be Lord of our lives.

A passage to live by

In seeking to follow the Lord in this way we come again to the main passage of scripture that we will be looking at as we study this topic. First, look once more at "*How can a young man keep his way pure? By living according to your word*" (Psalm 119:9). The word being talked about in this verse is the Word of God. Now, here is the passage from God's Word that we want to focus on in this study:

> "*Finally, brothers, we instructed you how to live in order to please God, as in fact you are living. Now we ask you and urge you in the Lord Jesus to do this more and more. For you know what instructions we gave you by the authority of the Lord Jesus. It is God's will that you should be holy; that you should avoid sexual immorality; that each of you should learn to control his own body in a way that is holy and honorable, not in passionate lust like the heathen, who do not know God; and that in this matter no one should wrong his brother or take advantage of him. The Lord will punish men for all such sins, as we have already told you and warned you. For God did not call us to be impure, but to live a holy life. Therefore, he who rejects this instruction does not reject man but God, who gives you his Holy Spirit. Now about brotherly love we do not need to write to you, for you yourselves have been taught by God to love each other. And in fact, you do love all the brothers throughout Macedonia. Yet we urge you, brothers, to do so more and more*"
> (I Thessalonians 4:1-10).

Purity is a blessing! Refuse to live it like it is a curse.

In looking at this passage, you can see the strong emphasis on living a pure and holy life. We will focus on different portions of this passage throughout this book, but right now we will provide you with an overview and will define several terms that will allow us to move forward together, knowing that we are speaking the same language.

First, know that what we are learning from the Bible is the truth. Jesus made it clear that those who knew and obeyed the truth would be set free! Purity is not a curse or a form of bondage. The message of purity is one of freedom and blessing. "*Blessed are the pure in heart, for they shall see God*" (Matthew 5:8). Too often we look at the command to be pure as if it were a curse. At best, we live it as simply something we must accept. Then we pray that we'll get married young, and we think that marriage will settle the purity issue. God's Word is truth. God calls purity a **blessing**! Are you willing to agree with God?

Pleasing God … it is possible!

"Finally, brothers, we instructed you how to live in order to please God, as in fact you are living. Now we ask you and urge you in the Lord Jesus to do this more and more. For you know what instructions we gave you by the authority of the Lord Jesus" (I Thessalonians 4:1).

This passage begins with the promise that we can live a life that is pleasing to God. In fact, we are told in this passage to live our lives in such a way that pleases God more and more. Thankfully we even have instructions on how we can do this. Unfortunately we often don't take the time to read the instructions which are clearly spelled out in the Bible.

Have you ever done the experiment in a science class where you are told to figure out a way to drop an egg from a height of one story or two or three and to do it in such a way that the egg does not break? It's not an easy task, but there are some ways in which this can be done. Most often, though, the egg breaks.

> *"There is a way that seems right to a man, but in the end it leads to death."*
>
> *Proverbs 14:12*

If that egg represents your heart, your life, and your purity, and you are looking at a splattered egg on the sidewalk, you know that shattered purity results in broken hearts and broken lives. Whether or not the egg survives depends solely on the design of the structure meant to protect it. An effective design preserves the egg; a faulty design allows it to break.

Upon what are you basing your design for relationships?

Dead end

"There is a way that seems right to a man, but in the end it leads to death" (Proverbs 14:12). Too often we find out the truth of this verse by experience. Think back on the experiment with the egg. If we gave you foolproof instructions which would guarantee saving the egg, instructions that if you followed to the letter would keep your egg from breaking, would you follow them?

Finally, brothers, we instructed you how to live in order to please God (I Thessalonians 4:1). God has given us His foolproof instructions for living that will not only keep us from breaking but will, instead, make our lives full and complete. He wants to reveal His will and design to you. In fact, He is showing His love and kindness to you right now simply because He has led you to read these truths at this moment.

Choose life

It is God's will that you should be sanctified: that you should avoid sexual immorality; (1 Thessalonians 4:3). Have you ever asked what God's will is for your life? Part of His will is for you to be holy and to avoid sexual immorality. He has stated that very clearly. How are you doing in this area? If you are not doing too well and yet you are asking God to show you His will for your life, you need to ask why God would reveal the will you don't know when you are not being obedient to the will that you already know?

"This day I call heaven and earth as witnesses against you that I have set before you life and death, blessings and curses. Now choose life, so that you and your children may live and that you may love the LORD your God, listen to his voice, and hold fast to him. For the LORD is your life..." (Deuteronomy 30:19-20).

God's will is that you choose life, not death. He has revealed His will and design to you concerning purity and holiness. His ways bring life. It is God's will that you should be holy.

Holy means whole me

When I ask people do you want to be holy, they usually grimace and say, "Well, I know that I should," as if they were being asked to take a distasteful medicine, maybe something like a mixture of battery acid, vinegar, and mayonnaise. When those same people are asked if they would like to be whole, complete, healthy in body, mind, and spirit, they respond "Well of course!" Most of us don't realize that holiness and wholeness are one and the same thing.

It is interesting to note that our English word *holy* derives from the Greek word *hal* which means hale, healthy, whole. Many people are searching for wholeness and peace. These characteristics can come only from God. Part of what holy means is to be whole in God, and He desires to give us this gift of wholeness. In Ephesians we are told to *"put on the new self, created to be like God in true righteousness and holiness"* (Ephesians 4:24). When we break God's laws, we live broken lives. *"They are darkened in their understanding and separated from the life of God because of the ignorance that is in them due to the hardening of their hearts"* (Ephesians 4:18). Holiness is about living the new life that God has called you to. It is a life that is both full and free.

Holy also means separation to God, to be set apart, to be sacred. Most of us want to feel that our life has purpose. Being holy means being set apart by God for a special purpose. To be holy is to be right in line with God's purposes for your life. You don't want to miss out on them. Too many people struggle with feeling as though their lives are empty and meaningless. To be holy means "whole me", set apart for Jesus' purposes today! You can begin right now to claim and live this complete life. Any other choice you make will result only in emptiness and frustration.

I see You or ICU

The word *holy* in its most basic form means *terrible shining*. This does not mean terrible as we may use the word to describe something bad, but the word really means to be *overwhelming*. This is a word used in reference to God, but it is also something that He calls his

> *"put on the new self, created to be like God in true righteousness and holiness."*
>
> *Ephesians 4:24*

people to. *"…so that you may become blameless and pure, children of God without fault in a crooked and depraved generation, in which you shine like stars in the universe as you hold out the word of life"* (Philippians 2:15).

If you think that the definition of the word *holy* means dull or boring, you need to take hold of a new definition, the word as God means it. *"Blessed are the pure in heart, for they shall see God"* (Matthew 5:8).

"Make every effort to live in peace with all men and to be holy; without holiness no one will see the Lord" (Hebrews 12:14).

Do you think purity and holiness are boring? Do you think seeing God would be boring? Notice that both verses quoted above have to do not only with purity, holiness, but also with seeing God. God wants to be real in your life; He wants to be powerful and active in making your life full, complete, and exciting. He is not a boring God!

If you were to do a short Bible study of people who have seen God and their responses, you would soon come to realize that a pure and holy life is anything but boring. Here are some references you can use to begin your study:

> Exodus 3:6
> Judges 13:20-22
> Isaiah 6:1-8
> Ezekiel 1:26-28
> Matthew 17:6-7
> Revelation 1:12-17

After you read these, we think you will agree that there is nothing dull or boring about seeing God. He hasn't changed. Relationship with Him is still as exciting and astounding as it was when these passages were written.

How far can I go?

If you are serious about living a pure and holy life, one question that you will likely ask is how the Bible defines holy living particularly in the area of sexual purity. Strictly by definition, sexual immorality (the biblical word is often *fornication)* means sexual intercourse or sexual activity between two people who are not married. Technically, the word *intercourse* means communication. So, we have to ask this question. Are you involved in sexual communication outside of marriage? This communication includes physical activity, but it also includes pornography, flirtatious behavior, and, in fact, sexual communication of any kind with someone or about someone to whom you are not married. In fact, according to the Bible, immorality means all sexual activity that is outside of God's prescribed boundaries. And God has clearly stated that sexual activity is pure and holy only when it is practiced within a marriage relationship.

Blessed are the pure in heart, for they shall see God.

Matthew 5:8

It's about pathetic relationships.

"My daughter will never date!" The angry words hissed from the father as he described his approach to managing his daughter's relationships. "She will ask us permission, the young man will inform us of his constant whereabouts. You do agree that dating is wrong don't you?" I smiled and calmly replied, "Sir, I am neither for nor against dating, but I am against pathetic relationships being formed." "What do you mean? You have to be against dating in today's world." Sound familiar? Today we are caught up in arguments over dating, courting, and ever other form of relationship development. True, about 98% of the dating going on today is pathetic, but we are missing a key point.

Whether teens are dating or not, they are forming relationships. A common question asked is how many teens have had a 16 year old requirement placed on them regarding 'dating'. The hands go up, and smiles drift across faces. Three follow up questions are then asked. First, "How many of you held hands with a member of the opposite sex apart from mom, dad, grandma or grandpa before you were 16 years old?" Over the years about 90% of those teens have said yes to that question. Second, "How many of you have kissed a member of the opposite sex apart from mom, dad, grandma or grandpa before you were 16 years old?" That percentage has hung in at about 75%. Third, "How many of you broke your parent's rule and went out on a date?" Only 30% say that they have been on a date. What's wrong with this picture? We must recognize that relationships are being developed and while teens are not necessarily 'dating' they are moving in a dangerous direction.

The concept of pathetic relationships is crucial to our understanding. While dating and courting need to be addressed we must recognize the need to evaluate relationships on all levels. As a young man I was not allowed to attend movies or go to dances, because of the bad things that were associated with them. However, 'praise God', my youth group organized hayrides and roller skating parties. At these events I watched, and occasionally participated in the formation of pathetic relationships. The fact is that we are all in the process of forming relationships. The question is, "Are they healthy or unhealthy?" An easy reference point is what we call "Seven Signs of a Pathetic Relationship".

We are all in the process of forming relationships. Are they healthy or pathetic?

1.   **Poor or no communication.**
        It is argumentative, doesn't listen and stays externally focused. It is not unusual to hear the words, "Everybody else is doing it."
2.   **Focus is on the physical. Seeks immediate gratification.**
        "I love you." It can come out of our mouths without even knowing what love is. In today's world the words lust and love need to be clearly differentiated. I encourage people to ask someone to define love for them when it escapes from their lips. Many young relationships use

love when they really mean lust. The major difference between love and lust is that love is always about 'giving', lust is always about 'taking'. Someone focused primarily on the physical will argue over the little things such as how far is too far. Finally, they do not grasp the concept of the progression of the physical relationship. The rule of progression says that whatever was done physically today becomes our reference point for tomorrow. In other words, if we held hands for the first time yesterday our reference point today is that we will hold hands. That progression characterizes relationships.

3. **Ignores significant others.**

Parents, friends, mentors, and other adults are avoided as much as possible. If conversations are required, eye contact is hard to maintain, and a lack of depth in the conversation is noticeable.

4. **Minimizes spiritual and mental needs.**

The other duties of life such as school, church activities, work, extra curricular activities at best do not improve, while there can be a marked worsening of efforts. Any confrontation of such performance is explained away by blaming others. Questions about learning and growth are not initiated by the person, and avoided if at all possible.

5. **Is primarily exclusive.**

"My friend can't even talk with me anymore. She only has time to be with her boyfriend." This statement has been heard thousands of time. Good relationships do not dominate, but rather open doors for improved relationships in other areas. One party often feels infringed upon if others try to continue their previous friendship. This often is evidenced in demands and anger directed to others. Other relationships are ignored or greatly diminished.

6. **Seeks out secret places, situations and circumstances.**

People can easily create right reasons for being in the wrong places, situations and circumstances. If the heart is seeking out ways to be alone for the wrong reasons it will find a place. Teens can wait until everyone else has gone to bed, look for opportunities when no one else will be at home, or simply finds the place where no one else will be. Good relationships look for opportunities to be open and upfront. The heart issue must be constantly examined by the young person desiring to do relationships right.

7. **Quickly justifies and defends actions.**

Many times individuals will adopt an offensive position to cover the wrongs. They will try to answer surface questions before the right questions are asked. If others persist in getting the proper questions asked the answers usually become short, brisk and defensive.

If we commit to knowing God, the issue of how far we can go sexually will, over a period of time, become crystal clear.

18

Caution: Relationships are being developed regardless of the terms we associate with them. Another father approached later in the same week as the 'never date' father. He had a son who was being approached by teenage girls who were being very bold in their suggestions and comments to this young man. Their conduct had all the signs of pathetic relationships. His words to his father were, "You can't believe some of the things they are saying!" He pointed one of the young ladies out to me. Later that day I saw the young woman with her father. Guess who he was? 'Never date' dad may have been keeping his daughter from dating, but she was in the process of developing pathetic relationships.

It's just like baseball.

Imagine for a minute that we are going to play baseball together. But after playing for just a few minutes, you realize that there is a problem because it seems that our definition of baseball is different than yours. We think that playing baseball means only catching fly balls. You're dumbfounded, and ask "How about hitting?"

"Uh, no."
"Running the bases?"
"Zip."
"Ground balls?"
"Zilch."
"Pitching?"
"Nada."

Pretty stupid, huh? You probably would be kind enough to explain to us that baseball is composed of a whole lot more than one activity. The game is made up of many interrelated parts.

"There's a lot more to it than you realize," you would patiently explain. We would be sure to thank you.

Sex is the same way. Some people think that sex is defined only by sexual intercourse. But that is a mistake. Just like baseball, it's a whole lot more than a single activity. Sex is made up of many interrelated parts. In fact, there's more to it than most of us realize. It sometimes involves things as simple as a touch, a spoken word, or a facial expression and, at other times activity as complete as sexual intercourse.

There is no passage in the Bible that defines how far you can go in a sexual relationship outside of marriage. The reason for that seeming omission is that God intends sexual expression to be contained solely inside the secure walls of a strong marriage. There is no other appropriate place for it. This is not because intimacy is so bad, but because it's so powerful, and God intends it to be a powerfully good. We will explore this more in depth in the chapter entitled Know God's Way.

God intends

intimacy

to be

'powerfully'

good!

The question, "How far can I go?" presupposes a dangerous idea. It seems to imply that the questioner wants to get as close to sin as possible without crossing the line. The correct question really is, "How close can I get to God?" If we commit to knowing God, the issue of how far we can go sexually will, over a period of time, become crystal clear.

Who's in control here, anyway?

"...each of you should learn to control his own body in a way that is holy and honorable, not in passionate lust like the heathen, who do not know God" (I Thessalonians 4:4).

What does it mean to control your body in a way that is holy and honorable? Have you ever been out of control? Bob Stone and Bob Palmer write that the Bible indicates that God's plan is that our sexual appetites should awaken gradually but be controlled until they are fulfilled and satisfied in a marriage relationship. The problem we face is that there is much in our world and in our lives which serves to threaten God's perfect plan.

Stone and Palmer continue, "In 1 Corinthians 7:1 the Bible says: *"It is not good for a man to touch a woman."* God gave the warning to the unmarried couple because he knew that touching would arouse sexual desires in both the man and the woman. Because God reserved sex for marriage, he cautions us not to arouse sexual desires in others that cannot be honorably gratified.

Let's go back to I Thessalonians 4:4. The first term that we need to define is *honorable*. My dictionary defines *honor* as, "a valuing by which the price is fixed." I like this definition because it suggests that you will not discount a person because you don't want to pay the price. You are not to treat them as if they are cheap goods like the heathen who do not know God. Why? Because you know Jesus. He is the one who paid the ultimate price for you—His life. *"Do you not know that your body is a temple of the Holy Spirit, who is in you, whom you have received from God? You are not your own; you were bought at a price. Therefore honor God with your body,"* (I Corinthians 6:19-20).

Are you honoring those around you? This does not just apply to members of the opposite sex. Put-downs and criticisms are other ways by which we can dishonor those around us. However, you can be a person who builds others up by honoring them in word (with your mouth) and in deed (with your body). You can be a source of blessing to those around you. *"Do not let any unwholesome talk come out of your mouths, but only what is helpful for building others up according to their needs, that it may benefit those who listen"* (Ephesians 4:29).

Another word in I Thessalonians 4:4 that we need to define is *passionate lust*. Passionate lust is to strongly desire to have what

The correct question is, "How close can I get to God?"

belongs to someone else and/or to engage in an activity which is morally wrong, especially with regards to sexuality. The verse above refers to the fact that *"heathen, who do not know God"* do these things. That tells us that if we belong to Christ, we need to act like it. Otherwise, we will be acting like those who do not even know God.

Taking advantage of the Golden Rule
"and that in this matter no one should wrong his brother or take advantage of him. The Lord will punish men for all such sins, as we have already told you and warned you" (I Thessalonians 4:6).

What is the Golden Rule? Even unbelievers acknowledge the value of this truth. It is one of the teachings for which Jesus is almost universally known. He said it this way, *"So in everything, do to others what you would have them do to you, for this sums up the Law and the Prophets"* (Matthew 7:12).

The Golden Rule serves as a guide for right behavior in all situations. My children recognize this immediately.

"How do you want your brother to talk to you?"

After an audible sigh, "Kindly."

"Well then how do you think that you should treat your brother?"

"Kindly."

It's that simple.

One of the great misunderstandings that we sometimes fall into is mistaking simple for easy. Elizabeth Elliot explains this well in her book *Passion and Purity*. "I'm always having to explain to people that when I say there is a simple answer I do not necessarily mean there is an easy answer. It's easy enough to understand—in other words, *it's simple*. But doing it is just plain hard. There is always that fundamental conflict going on: the good I want to do fighting the evil I don't want to do and the desire that seems to be so good in itself versus the deeper desire to love my Master above all others."

Realizing that this is true, how do you take advantage of the Golden Rule in your relationships rather than taking advantage of others in your relationships? *"So in everything (including your relationships), do to others what you would have them do to you"* (Matthew 7:12).

Look at it this way. We are sure that you want your marriage to be special, unique, pure, and glorifying to God. If you are called to be married, then your spouse-to-be is walking around on this planet right now. How far do you want your future wife or husband to be going with others physically or sexually right now?

> *"So in everything, do to others what you would have them do to you..."*
>
> *Matthew 7:12*

Do unto others around you now what you would have those around your future mate do to him or her. Don't have a double standard.

We ignore the rest of the I Thessalonians verse at our peril. It says, *"The Lord will punish men for all such sins, as we have already told you and warned you."* I know many people who have experienced the punishment for these sins: broken lives, broken relationships, and broken hearts. God can heal and forgive (We will talk more about this in Chapter 9), but there are consequences for sin. Committing sexual sin is like bungee jumping off the Grand Canyon…without the bungee. Imagine that the guy lived through the jump. With a broken and bruised body he cries out to God, "Why didn't you save me… why did you let this happen?" Can you think of an appropriate reply to this person? There is one in the Bible. It says, *"A man's own folly ruins his life, yet his heart rages against the LORD."* (Proverbs 19:3). We will revisit this concept in the chapter entitled Know God's View. How much better it is to accept the directives God has so plainly given. How much better it is to seek relationship with Him instead of pursuing relationships with others outside the boundaries God has set.

Blessed are the impure?
"For God did not call us to be impure, but to live a holy life," (I Thessalonians 4:7) and *"Blessed are the pure in heart, for they shall see God,"* (Matthew 5:8).

Do you believe that the statements given above are true? We hope that you do because they come directly out of God's Word.

Purity means clean, unblemished, untainted. It means innocence, chastity, and lacking contamination. It is easy to think of purity as something that doesn't matter that much; in fact, as we mentioned earlier, purity to you might sound as if it is kind of boring.

It was Saturday night and my wife was away from home teaching a Creative Memories class. Of course, being the caring father that I am, I already had the dinner menu planned. It was men's night (this was before the birth of my beautiful daughter) at our house, and for my sons and me that meant pizza for dinner topped off with ice cream and followed by games. We were hungry and money was tight, but we figured that one pizza should cover us three guys and a toddler. Unfortunately, it wasn't enough. Before we knew it, the pizza was gone—all except the one piece on my son Dillon's plate. My son Alex and I both ogled it as we wiped our slavering mouths. You see, Dillon is a grazer with a small but constant appetite—he doesn't really eat as much as he refuels, and his tank was just about topped off. Alex and I, on the other hand, love food and we thank God for it as a good thing in and of itself. We looked over at my youngest son Lucas and laughed—he wasn't even a contender. Before he even became aware that another slice was available, it would be gone. Then Alex and I eyed each other. Sitting at Dillon's elbow, I had Alex effectively boxed out and he knew it. He gave me a look of appeal—perhaps we could share.

We waited to hear Dillon say the sought after words, "Dad, I'm not hungry anymore." But Dillon didn't say those words, Instead, he said, "Dad, I don't feel so good."

I should have noted the color of his face at this point, but I just said, "That's okay, Dill, just go rest."

As he made a move to leave the table, I made my move for the pizza. But at the same time I heard a terrible retching noise "Bbbuuuiiiccckkk." The reddish purple liquid fell in splattering semi-congealed blobs on that once perfect and pure piece of pepperoni pizza, as the stench from my son's bile and semi-digested food assaulted us like the aftershock of an earthquake. Appetite gone.

Would you want to eat that piece of pizza? Neither did I. In fact, some of you are having a hard time just reading this even without the benefit of having the whole sensory experience. So what does this crazy illustration have to do with purity? Everything.

Impurity is a stench in the nostrils of God. He didn't create us for impurity, but for purity. You see, purity matters. It is beautiful to God and to us. We are attracted to purity. Impurity, on the other hand, takes something of value and ruins it, making it not only worthless, but also despised. God does not want us to experience the consequences of impurity. In fact, He wants so much for us to experience purity that He gave His life to pay the price of redeeming us from impurity. *"'Come now, let us reason together' says the LORD. 'Though your sins are like scarlet, they shall be as white as snow; though they are red as crimson, they shall be like wool',"* (Isaiah 1:18) God has taken the stain and contamination from us.

Are you beginning to see that purity is a blessing and not a curse? Too often we miss out on abundant life because we fall for a lie instead of standing on the truth. Jesus made it clear that those who knew and obeyed His truth would be set free! The message of purity is one of freedom, blessing, and joy. *"Blessed are the pure in heart, for they shall see God."* (Matthew 5:8). Our hope is that those who believe in Jesus would agree with Him that purity is a blessing, not a curse.

The heart of the matter
"If we confess our sins, he is faithful and just and will forgive us our sins and purify us from all unrighteousness" (1 John 1:9).

"For the grace of God that brings salvation has appeared to all men. It teaches us to say 'No' to ungodliness and worldly passions, and to live self-controlled, upright and godly lives in this present age, while we wait for the blessed hope—the glorious appearing of our great

Impurity is a stench in the nostrils of God.

God and Savior, Jesus Christ, who gave himself for us to redeem us from all wickedness and to purify for himself a people that are his very own, eager to do what is good" (Titus 2:11-14).

The heart of the matter is that purity is a matter of the heart. Where does one get a pure heart? Purity is not something we can earn. A person could be a virgin until his or her wedding day and still be impure. Conversely, a person may have committed sexual sins and still be pure in God's eyes. How?

"The LORD does not look at the things man looks at. Man looks at the outward appearance, but the LORD looks at the heart" (I Samuel 16:7).

We can only be pure in a relationship with Jesus. Our heart is renewed when we receive forgiveness of sins by our faith in Jesus, just as this verse in Acts points out, *"…for he purified their hearts by faith."* (Acts 15:9). Your heart is made pure by our faith in Jesus who has promised to give you a clean heart.

This promise is not a license to sin. It simply means that we are sinners in need of a Savior. Once we receive the much-needed forgiveness Jesus offers, He plants in us His Holy Spirit and, with that, a new desire to do what is right by His power. It's not that the struggle will be over, but with our new heart, we have been given the power to overcome temptation and we have been given the desire to please our heavenly Father. Those two motivations combined enable us to live the life of purity and holiness that God requires.

I asked a young man who had struggled greatly with his purity in the past how he was doing. "I've been real pure. No one will go out with me."

He was missing the point. He was assuming that the absence of opportunity meant the presence of purity. Purity is an inward reality that leads to outward behaviors. It is not lifestyle change that comes by self-denial and hard work; it is a supernatural work of the Holy Spirit creating in us a desire to be like Christ. Purity has to happen inside before it will show on the outside.

What is love?
"Now about brotherly love we do not need to write to you, for you yourselves have been taught by God to love each other. And in fact, you do love all the brothers throughout Macedonia. Yet we urge you, brothers, to do so more and more" (I Thessalonians 4:9-10).

If you want a full accounting of what God defines as love, read 1 Corinthians 13 from beginning to end. God says that love means commitment; it means doing what is in the best interest of another; it means never giving up; it means thinking the best about someone even when they are not treating you very well.

Love is a word that is so often used, but just about as often misunderstood. A past beer commercial was famous for the line, "I love you, man." What was obvious in the commercial is that the speaker really meant, "I want your beer."

Love, as used in our society, is not considered eternal as the writers of old had dreamed; instead, it is treated as a feeling that is temporary and fleeting. Recently while participating in a silence and solitude retreat, I walked up a long stairway to a deck overlooking Lake Michigan. On the ascent, I noticed several items of graffiti avowing "love forever and ever" by various individuals. On the descent, I stopped to study them in more detail. There were nine inscriptions. Of those nine, three individuals had already returned, crossed out one name and replaced it with the new 'love' of their lives. Scary, isn't it? The person you think you love today may not be the person you love tomorrow. It takes time for love to grow and to be recognized as the I Corinthians 13 love that God desires for each of us. Don't hurry into a love relationship. Let God show you when you are there.

To see or not to see

Remember the verse in Matthew 5:8, *"Blessed are the pure in heart for they shall see God."* Purity is a blessing that gives us vision. It opens our eyes to the presence of God. The more we are like Him, the better we see Him and the closer we relate to Him.

Impurity blinds us! Have you lost a sense of God's presence in your Life? Maybe it's time to check you purity level. Those who have pure hearts are blessed or happy because they will see God! Not just in the future. You can know His life and His presence now! But you have to have a pure heart before you will see Him up close and personal.

Purity is not an option.

"Nothing impure will ever enter it, nor will anyone who does what is shameful or deceitful, but only those whose names are written in the Lamb's book of life" (Revelation 21:27).

"Make every effort to live in peace with all men and to be holy; without holiness no one will see the Lord" (Hebrews 12:14).

Holy living is God's will for us and is His calling upon our lives. Holiness means to be set apart, without sin, Christ-like, and consecrated. What are we to be set apart for? For and to God Himself. We are His. He has special plans for us. We are to be set apart from all that is sinful. We are to be set apart to His service and to do His will. Once we are consecrated in that way, our lives will be different. We will live in a way that brings honor to God's holy name and with conduct befitting a child of God.

We have to remember that pure living is not an option. Let's return to our central passage. *"Therefore, he who rejects this instruction does not reject man but God, who gives you his Holy Spirit."*

Love is a word that is so often used, but just about as often misunderstood.

(I Thessalonians 4:8). To reject this instruction is to reject God! When we choose to disobey a clear command of God, we are choosing to live in open rebellion to Him. That is our choice. As for me, I choose God and choose to follow whatever He commands.

A blessing that keeps us sane.
"The mind of sinful man is death, but the mind controlled by the Spirit is life and peace;" (Romans 8:6).

"Furthermore, since they did not think it worth while to retain the knowledge of God, he gave them over to a depraved mind, to do what ought not to be done" (Romans 1:28).

Impurity is insanity; it is to believe a lie and to live according to that lie. God is telling you the truth when He says that the pure in heart will see God, when He says that a mind controlled by the Holy Spirit will bring life and peace, and when He says that you are too be holy as He is holy. Satan is filling your mind with lies when he tells you that just this once won't matter, that you shouldn't deprive yourself of certain indulgences, and that there won't be any consequences for the sinful choices you make. Listening to Satan is insane. Listening to God is life, peace, joy, and fulfillment. What choice will you make?

"The mind of sinful man is death, but the mind controlled by the Spirit is life and peace;"

Romans 8:6

Journal Page

Take Action

Pray asking God to identify a statement and/or scripture that was meaningful to you in this chapter.

On your journal page, write this statement or scripture passage as well as any other thoughts or feelings you have in response to what you are learning.

Know God's Word

Memory Verse

"Finally, brothers, we instructed you how to live in order to please God, as in fact you are living. Now we ask you and urge you in the Lord Jesus to do this more and more" (1 Thessalonians 4:1).

Read 1 Thessalonians 4:1-8.

In the space provided below, rewrite 1 Thessalonians 4:1-8 in your own words. Try not to use any of the actual words from the Bible text. For example you might begin verse 3 by writing, "Our Father desires..." instead of "It is God's will..."

Day by Day

Day 1

List the instructions that are given in 1 Thessalonians 4:1-8.

What are the purposes of the instructions given in verses 1, 2, and 8?

For those of you who are living according to these instructions (even if only feebly), be encouraged: You are pleasing God. Why do you think Paul still gives these instructions if his readers are already living in agreement with them?

How do you do this *more and more* as instructed in verse 2?

What is the result of living according to these instructions (see verse 1)? Is this your desire? Explain your answer.

Rate your desire to please God on a scale of 1 to 10 (with 10 being the highest).

Pray now and ask God to increase your desire to live a life pleasing to Him.

"Finally, brothers, we instructed you how to live in order to please God, as in fact you are living. Now we ask you and urge you in the Lord Jesus to do this more and more."
   1 Thessalonians 4:1

Know God's Word

Read 1 Thessalonians 4:1-8.

Do you want to know God's will for your life?

According to verse 3, what is God's will for you life?

Day by Day

Day 2

What do you think it means to be holy? If you have a dictionary available, it may be helpful to look up the word.

Why do people struggle with being holy?

As clearly as possible, define sexual immorality.

How do you avoid sexual immorality?

List two things you could do to live a more holy life.

Know God's Word

Read 1 Thessalonians 4:1-8 and Matthew 5:27-30.

What point is Jesus making in Matthew 5:27-28?

1 Samuel 16:7 says *"Man looks at the outward appearance, but the Lord looks at the heart."* How is this verse related to what Jesus is saying in the Matthew passage cited above?

Matthew 5:30 tells us that if something, even something precious to us, causes us to sin, we should cut it off. What are some of the behaviors and attitudes in your life that cause you to sin?

How can you cut these off with God's help?

Day by Day

Day 3

Return to the last two questions in the Day 2 study and make any changes or additions you can think of.

Know God's Word

Read 1 Thessalonians 4:1-10.

What does it mean to control one's body in a way that is holy and honorable?

Imagine a young man were going to date your younger sister, whom you love greatly. He wants to do what's right so he asks you, "What does it mean to control my body in a way that is holy and honorable and not in passionate lust?" What answer would you give him?

What is lust?

What is love?

Know God's Word

Read 1 Thessalonians 4:1-8 and Matthew 7:12.

How do you see Matthew 7:12 pertaining to your relationships right now?

You want your marriage to be special, unique, pure, and glorifying to God. If you are called to be married, then your husband or wife-to-be is walking around on this planet right now. How far do you want your future marriage partner to be going with others sexually at this time?

Do you want your future spouse to save himself or herself for you?

What does the term, "saving yourself" mean to you?

Are you saving yourself for your future marriage partner?

Do to others around you now what you would have others do around your future mate. Don't have a double standard.

Pray for your future spouse, that he or she would be honoring God with all his/her being and pray that you would do the same.

Day by Day

Day 5

Know God's Word

Review and reflect.

Review the verse for the week and the verses used in all five previous days of devotions.

What are the three biggest lessons you learned from this week's materials?

For each of those lessons, write a one-sentence statement explaining why it impressed you.

How does this material relate to staying pure and holy?

I Thessalonians 4:3a says, *"It is God's will that we should be holy."* Notice that this is not a question; it is a statement of fact There is no doubt about what God's will for our lives is. He wants us to be holy.

If it is God's will for us to be holy, then there must be excellent reasons why. God does not tell us to do things that are not in our best interest. One youth approached me tentatively years ago, and asked what reasons I could give for why he should stay pure and holy. With a sheepish look on his face he said, "My friends laughed at me and asked why I would do anything as stupid as to not have sex. I couldn't think of anything to say, except that God says so."

Could it be true that people know the what (be holy), but not the why? As we searched for the whys, we observed that after only a few minutes of discussing that very difficult question, teens were coming up with some excellent answers. After one session, one young man cried out, "There are more good reasons to stay pure than there are not to!" For many, finding the reasons for purity and holiness is a life changing discovery.

Over the years, teens have developed a list of over 25 reasons why it is wise to take a stand for purity and holiness. That list, as we will show you below, has been divided into three categories: physical, mental/emotional, and spiritual. While the reasons listed may overlap into more than one of these categories, this compilation serves to remind us that when God says, "Be holy" there are good reasons for that command.

Physical Reasons

There will be no sexual/physical comparisons later in life.
You will be the best lover your spouse has ever known.
You will be free from the danger of sexually transmitted diseases (STDs).
Sex will be an area reserved as special for your spouse.
You will be free from unwanted pregnancy.
You will not be sinning against your body.
You will live with a reduced threat of abuse.

Emotional/Mental Reasons

Pure living protects your reputation.
Your life will stand out as an example to others.
You will not have to live with guilt feelings.

You will avoid emotional scars and pain.
You will build self-respect and confidence.
Purity will not promote a 'give me' attitude.
Moral purity helps to prevent addictions.
You will avoid destroyed emotions.
Purity allows real relationships to develop untainted by ulterior motives.

Spiritual Reasons

Purity is God's will, it is God's call on your life.
God commands it.
You will learn to say "no" to evil.
Purity prevents obstacles in your walk with God.
Moral living provides opportunities to witness to others.
There is a blessing promised for obedience in this area of your life.
Purity allows you to live under God's special design.
Your faith will increase as you see God work out the details of your life.
Obedience avoids punishment.
Practicing self-control is a spiritual discipline that draws you closer to God.
Obedience pleases your heavenly Father and will be rewarded.

Physical reasons

Let's talk about each one of these areas for a few moments. Physical reasons for purity usually resonate with females faster and more deeply than with the males. Unfortunately, in our society it is still true that a man who goes to bed with several women is known as a stud, macho man, or some kind of hero. A woman taking the same course of action is known as a whore or slut. Too often, it is the female's responsibility to say, "Stop". This should not be the case with Christians. Young men need to be challenged to take their stand for purity and to lead their partner by godly example.

Unwanted pregnancies, STD's, and physical or sexual abuse head the list of physical problems that result from impure activities and, thereby, give us strong arguments for leading a life of sexual purity. While some, even in Christian circles, have turned to abortion as their answer to unplanned pregnancy, the emotional scars such a decision leave are just now beginning to surface. The guilt and shame for many quickly move pregnancy from just a physical reason into the emotional/mental column. The STD rates fluctuate from survey to survey, but even the most optimistic studies are filled with great pain and suffering. Date rape, sex drugs, and physical abuse are on the rise among the teen dating scene. While even the most innocent individual can be trapped in a bad situation, it is well established that wrong relationships lead more rapidly to devastating results both physically and emotionally.

"It is God's will that we should be holy."

1 Thessalonians 4:3a

In our society it seems that sexual promiscuity is almost accepted as the norm. The concept of multiple partners leads to comparisons between them. Yet, in God's plan, which allows only one partner, there is no one else to whom to compare. I've heard stories of men who, in a moment of deep affection, have called their wives by an ex-flame's name. Needless to say, the temperature in the room dropped quickly. By living life God's way, your spouse will be the best (and only) lover you will ever know. Some will rack this up as too simplistic. However, ordering a pizza, buying a car, or sitting in a thousand couches prior to purchasing one of them do not compare to the importance and eternal rewards for entering into a godly relationship. You don't find your life's partner by trial and error.

Emotional/mental reasons

Most people will agree in theory that there is a deeper side to humans than a physical body. However, we seem to spend a bunch of time stressing the physical aspects of our lives while ignoring the deeper issues. I once visited a men's college basketball locker room. On the board was a list of college coeds with a description of physical activities they would perform. I shuddered to think of the thousands of dollars some family had invested in advancing their daughter's mind, only to have her be known on campus for her body.

Each person builds a reputation. Through work ethic, contacts, and experience we become known. Most people desire to be respected and to be known in a positive light. Characteristics such as honest, hard working, humorous, trustworthy, caring and understanding top the list of qualities that one would desire in their future spouse. Proverbs 22:1 says, *"A good name is more desirable than great riches; to be esteemed is better than silver or gold."* Choices we make in our conduct put our reputation at stake. People desirous of a good reputation will take steps to protect it. As we develop good reputations, our opportunities to be positive examples to others grow. We hear so much talk about role models among athletes and entertainers. The greatest need today is for Christians to take a stand where they are and become those role models to their peers and to younger kids looking up to them on a day-to-day basis. You need to know as young people that you can step up and provide an example for others to follow.

> *"A good name is more desirable than great riches; to be esteemed is better than silver or gold."*
>
> *Proverbs 22:1*

Many times we have seen young people busting at the seams with joy as they relate how they withstood pressure and did what was right. They are living examples to show that, as you learn to obey God's Word, your confidence and respect for yourself will grow. During my tenure in the public schools as a counselor, it was not unusual for a troubled student to inform me that the so-called 'good kids' were doing things that would shock me. When I asked if there were other students whom they respected, they would direct me to students I knew to be Christians. They were not always the most popular, but other students did notice that they lived life somewhat differently and, for that, the Christian students were respected.

Guilt feelings, scars, hurts, and becoming trapped all fit into the mental/emotional reason category listed above. David addresses this kind of emotional pain in a prayer of repentance after his adulterous rendezvous with Bathsheba. Once he recognized the depth of his sin, he wrote, *"When I kept silent my bones wasted away through my groaning all day long. For day and night your hand was heavy upon me; my strength was sapped as in the heat of summer. Then I acknowledged my sin to you and did not cover up my iniquity. I said, 'I will confess my transgressions to the Lord' --- and you forgave the guilt of my sin"* (Psalm 51:3-5). Making right decisions today prevents guilt feelings tomorrow. The good news is that God is more concerned about where we are going than about where we have been. David realized his past wrong, confessed it, received God's forgiveness and healing, and then moved forward.

In a world that says 'me first', we must develop a Philippians 2:3 attitude. *"Do nothing out of selfish ambition or vain conceit, but in humility consider others better than yourself."* An excellent reason to stand in purity and holiness is to avoid that 'me first' attitude that leads to emptiness. Instead you begin to look at your date as your friend and as someone whom you consider valuable and worthy to be honored with pure and holy consideration.

Spiritual reasons

The deepest of the areas of reasons we have given above is the spiritual one. But that area also can be the hardest to understand. The answer we begin with in declaring our commitment to purity and holiness is that God says so. That is an excellent reason. Whenever God commands something, we know that it is in our best interest to obey. Being willing to obey just because God expects it not only enables us to learn to build godly relationships, but also becomes an opportunity to increase our faith, to learn the joys of obedience, to practice self-discipline, and to be presented opportunities to witness to others.

In addition to the growth we will experience through simple obedience, there are other benefits. Those include having no barriers between us and God and enjoying a life of blessing while avoiding the negative consequences of disobedience. God always has been, and always will be true to His Word. If He promises it, you can count on it. And He has promised a life of joy and blessing to those who are willing to obey His commands.

Remember back to the question posed earlier asking why you would you do something as stupid as denying yourself sex. Wouldn't it be powerful if you, as a young person committed to God, would long to have that question thrown your way? As soon as the words of the inquirer were out of his mouth, you could answer, "I choose to live that way because it teaches me obedience, it teaches me how to practice self-control, and I can live a guilt-free and happy life." That would be only the beginning of what you could say! After going

"Do nothing out of selfish ambition or vain conceit, but in humility consider others better than yourself."

Philippians 2:3

through the 25 or so reasons, you would end by asking, "Any other questions?"

We are convinced that if the reasons we are discussing were understood and shared, not in arrogance but in a confident humility, the questioner would respond with, "Wow, I never thought of it that way before!"

For too long we have lived out purity and holiness apologetically. We shrink back when questioned and confronted because we do not understand or really believe right down to our toes that it is the best life to live. Instead, we live in purity almost as if such a choice is a penalty rather than a blessing. When God says, *"Blessed are the pure in heart,"* He means it. Pure and holy living is a blessing to be enjoyed, not a curse to be endured. Don't let anyone teach you that this is our cross to bear when you know that it is a blessing that needs to be claimed and then lived out victoriously.

The foundations you are establishing right now will affect you for the rest of your life. The road to purity and holiness does not end at marriage. While, the issue of sexuality is a hot topic when you are in your dating years, the decision for purity and holiness is a lifelong act of obedience. If we address purity and holiness biblically as young people, the questions associated with sexuality both now and in the future will take on a proper perspective. We need to agree with God, call purity a blessing as He does, and choose live our lives His way.

Pure and holy living is a blessing to be enjoyed, not a curse to be endured.

Dig Deeper: Know God's Reasons

Finally, brothers, we instructed you how to live in order to <u>please God</u>...It is <u>God's will</u> that you should be sanctified: (1 Thessalonians 4:1, 3 emphasis added).

According to this passage, what's the first reason to be pure and holy?

There are better reasons to be pure and holy than there are to be impure and unholy.

In this chapter, we have explored reasons to stay pure. In the chart below fill out as many reasons as you can recall from your reading and add any that you can think of on your own. Feel free to check back in the chapter if you need to jog your memory.

SPIRITUAL

EMOTIONAL/MENTAL

PHYSICAL

Journal Page

Take Action
Pray asking God to identify a statement and/or scripture that was meaningful to you in this chapter.

On your journal page, write this statement or scripture passage as well as any other thoughts or feelings you have in response to what you are learning.

Know God's Reasons

Memory Verse

It is <u>God's will</u> that you should be sanctified: that you should avoid sexual immorality; (1 Thessalonians 4:3 emphasis added).

Read 1 Thessalonians 4:1-8.

As we did in Dig Deeper, list below as many reasons as you can think of for staying pure and holy. Some reasons could pertain to more than one section, so list them where you think they best fit. Has your list changed from the one you completed earlier? How? Why?

We will return to this section throughout the course, so keep it handy.

<u>SPIRITUAL</u>

<u>EMOTIONAL/MENTAL</u>

<u>PHYSICAL</u>

Know God's Reasons

Read Proverbs 14:12 and Isaiah 53:6.

Rewrite these verses in your own words.

Write down modern examples of these verses.

What happens to us if we follow our ways instead of God's ways?

How might these verses apply to our views of sexuality and relationships?

According to Isaiah 53:6, how can we go astray in relationships?

Day by Day

Day 2

Know God's Reasons

Read John 14:15-24.

According to verse 15, if you love Jesus what will you do?

Day by Day

Day 3

According to verse 24, if you don't love Jesus what will you do?

How obedient are you in the area of sexual purity?

What do verses 21 and 23 say about what Jesus does for those who love Him?

Mother Theresa writes in the foreword of **A Plea for Purity** as follows: "To be pure, to remain pure, can only come at a price, the price of knowing God and of loving him enough to do his will. He will always give us the strength we need to keep purity as something beautiful for God. Purity is the fruit of prayer...A pure heart is the carrier of God's love, and where there is love, there is unity, joy, and peace."

Know God's Reasons

Read Psalm 19:7-14.

What are we told in this passage about the law of the Lord?

What are the promises given in verse 11?

How would you rate the words of your mouth?

What about the meditations of your heart?

What do you think is pleasing in the sight of the Lord?

Return to Day 1 and see if you can add any more reasons to your chart.

Know God's Reasons

Read Psalm 51.

This is David's prayer after acknowledging his sin with Bathsheba. In verse 2, what does he say is ever before him?

Day by Day

Day 5

What are the feelings that David is expressing in this psalm?

What kind of heart does David want in as he describes in verse 10?

Why do you think that he wants this kind of heart?

What kind of heart do you desire? Why?

Can you think of any reasons to add to your list based on this passage? Go ahead and add them now.

Know God's Reasons

Review and reflect.

Review the verse for the week and all five previous days of devotions.

What are the three biggest lessons you learned from this week's materials?

For each of those lessons, write a one-sentence statement explaining why it impressed you.

Day by Day

Day 6

How does this material relate to staying pure and holy?

CHAPTER 3   KNOW GOD'S VIEW

"What do you see?"

I was trying hard to see something, to make sense out of this mess in front of me.

"A painting done by a child in a strait jacket?" I asked.

"Uh, no." My small group laughed as a fellow student diagnosed me as being repressed. Using some ink smeared pages, we were experimenting with various diagnostic techniques as part of a college psychology class at Michigan State University. I later realized that the way I saw those pictures during that time in my life is a lot like the way people see relationships. Mysterious. Messy. Confusing. Blurry. We say love is blind. Sometimes our view of relationships is such that I think we have it in both eyes!

How do you view relationships? Your perspective on relationships will have everything to do with how you approach them. But there's an even more important question. What is God's view of relationships? How does He see human interactions? What did He create them to be? What are His purposes in joining us together with others? If anyone sees things clearly, we know that Jesus does, and He wants to give us His vision.

Focus on His family.
"For this reason I kneel before the Father, from whom his whole family in heaven and on earth derives its name" (Ephesians 3: 14-15).

"This, then, is how you should pray: 'Our Father in heaven, hallowed be your name," (Matthew 6:9).

"...and that in this matter no one should wrong their brother/ sister or take advantage of them. For God will punish men for all such sins, as we have already told you and warned you..." (1 Thessalonians 4:5).

God created you to fit in. He designed you for belonging. Unfortunately, for many of us this concept is as foreign as speaking Tunisian. The connectedness you so strongly desire seems so elusive. However, take heart. You can experience these relational truths starting today. It all begins with your point of view. Let's take a look at these things through God's eyes.

According to the verses above, our primary relationship with God is not based on any of these models:

Employer/Employee
Teacher/Student
Agent/Client
Doctor/Patient
Master/Slave
Creator/Creation

God wants our primary relationship to Him to be Father/Son or Father/Daughter. Our heavenly Father teaches us that the foundation of all our relationships is family. When we become children of God, we enter into His family through His Son, Jesus. Because He loves you so much, God desires for you to know Him as Father. The blessing of this is evident in the relational pairs shown above. Each of the relationships in this list can be terminated. Each of them can be cold and can lack intimacy. Your employer can fire you. Your teacher this year will probably not be your teacher next year. A patient can choose a new doctor. A master may own a slave all his life, but never have a warm, intimate relationship with him.

God desires to have a relationship with you that is secure. To prove that, He has described Himself as your Father. Your employer may change, but your father never will. In spite of changes in your life or his, your earthly father will always be your father. It's a biological fact. God is your eternal father, a father who will never leave you or forsake you (Hebrews 13:5), a father who is as close as your next breath. God wants us to view our relationships with Himself and with other Christians first and foremost as family relationships. That is the best way He can communicate to us the security of the relationship and convey to us a sense of belonging that will never change.

As for intimacy, God created it and He embodies the word that we use for it: Love. *"And so we know and rely on the love God has for us. God is love"* (I John 4:16). God is love, and He wants you to know Him as the great love of your life. Of all the types of relationships that God could have with you, He chose to characterize it with love. He wants to have a love relationship with you. He is your loving father. In fact, when Jesus was asked to identify the greatest commandment he replied, *"Love the Lord your God with all your heart and with all your soul and with all your mind"* (Matthew 22:37). Our relationship with God is all about love – His for us and, as we grow, ours for Him as well.

The prayer that Jesus taught us to pray begins "Our Father." I always thought that was a funny way to start it. He could have said "My Father", but because He wants us to have a personal relationship with the Father just as He does, He made sure He included us in the opening words of this personal prayer. But then I realize that spiritual life is about more than just Jesus and me. When I enter into the family of God, I am not an only child. The Lord wants me to keep this in the forefront of my mind and heart. When I became His child, I was adopted into a family with a multitude of brothers and sisters. And He expects me to treat them all as members of the family.

I frequently pass a billboard that tells me "It's all about you." This announcement represents a self-centered philosophy that often follows us right into the church. Jesus wanted us to be clear that He is offering us a life where it's not just about us. Jesus wants us to be clear that the life He is offering is fulfilling **because** it's not just about us. He teaches us that real life is gained only by giving it away. He says, *"For whoever wants to save his life will lose it, but whoever loses his life for me will find it"* (Matthew 16:25).

Our Father desires us to view our relationships with one another as His children. We are brothers and sisters in Christ. We are all loved by our heavenly Father and He expects that we will love each other in the same way that He loves us. It's His view and, because it is His, it needs to be ours, too!

Corrected vision.

I recently had an eye exam. I presented an interesting problem for the optometrist. He could not understand how I had gone my whole life without glasses. I should have been in need of them from a young age. He concluded that my brain had been "turning off" one of my eyes so that I would not have double vision. "However," he made clear to me, "for proper depth perception you need two eyes."

The same is true of our relationships. If we see them only through one lens, the lens of physical perspective, we lose the ability for relational depth. This distorted vision comes when we neglect the second lens, the eye of the spirit. When we use both perspectives, we see a whole relationship – one that is healthy, growing, and deeply spiritual. The Bible gives clear direction on this matter. *"So from now on we regard no-one from a worldly point of view. Though we once regarded Christ in this way, we do so no longer"* (II Corinthians 5:16). We need to have our vision corrected. We need to see each other as brothers and sisters. In doing so, the whole relationship picture comes into clear focus.

Reject vs. accept.

As you enter the factory, you know that you are in a dream. The place is dark and the anxiety that surrounds you feels like a vise on your heart. It is tight, cold, and heavy. Ahead you see a conveyer belt. You see the belt plodding along eerily as it leads to two destinations. However, instead of moving toys or car parts, it's full of people. In fact, as your realization comes into perspective, you notice that one of those people is **you**! You see yourself approaching a fork in the belt where there is a great deal of noise and screaming. There is a person you know sitting at the Lever of Judgment. You're pretty sure that this person doesn't like you. So you try to think of something you can say to make him like you.

"Love the Lord your God with all your heart and with all your soul and with all your mind."

Matthew 22:37

As you get closer to the Lever of Judgment, you can see a sign off to the left that reads, "Rejected". Beyond that sign, you see people piled in a container. It is a dirty place full of depressed and anguished souls. Off to the right, you notice another sign that says, "Accepted". The place beyond that sign looks a little cleaner, but the people there look even more afraid, if that is possible. Then you see the reason. Even those who are in the accepted pile on this conveyer are just put on another belt with a different person standing at the next Lever of Judgment. It seems that the belts and the judgments go on forever. In your dream, you realize that you are coming to the Lever of Judgment so you start yelling to yourself: "Get off the belt. Get off the belt." The boy at the lever looks at you and smirks. "Get off the belt!" and you wake with a start.

This dream is an illustration of the world's way of doing relationships. Every encounter is a new chance to reject and to be rejected. Why? Well, when we think this way, we base our relationships on performance and upon what others can do for us. Are they popular enough in our group? Does their appearance fit with our group? Do they have the right interests? Are their grade good enough?

> *"So from now on we regard no-one from a worldly point of view. Though we once regarded Christ in this way, we do so no longer."*
>
> **II Corinthians 5:16**

This is not God's way. God's way teaches us to receive everyone, loving and appreciating them for who they are, *"Do not rebuke an older man harshly, but exhort him as if he were your father. Treat younger men as brothers, older women as mothers, and younger women as sisters, with absolute purity"* (1 Timothy 5:1,2). When we place other people on the conveyer belt heading toward judgment, we place ourselves on it as well. *""Stop judging others, and you will not be judged. For others will treat you as you treat them. Whatever measure you use in judging others, it will be used to measure how you are judged"* (Matthew 7:1-2 NLT).

The conveyer belt method discards meaningful relationships that look to the real person inside, made in the very image of God's spirit, emotion, and mind, and, instead, settles for a small world of "acceptable" acquaintances. God in His wisdom knows that it would be our tendency to behave this way. He also knows that this heart attitude wrecks our potential for real intimate relationship in which we can give and receive love that isn't tainted by mixed motives, appearance, popularity, and performance. When we choose the world's views, we lose. Having God's view improves our relationships!

Purpose-driven relationships — WHATEVER?

"Each one should use whatever gift he has received to serve others, faithfully administering God's grace in its various forms so that in all things God may be praised through Jesus Christ. To him be the glory and the power for ever and ever. Amen" (I Peter 4:10-11).

Where do we go wrong? Do you know what God's purpose is for your relationships? The problem usually begins right here. We either don't know or don't live out God's purposes for our relationships. Imagine freshman Joe is going to senior high youth group for the first time. Before him, as he walks in, is a table filled with his favorite pizza and standing around it are the most popular seniors in the group. Before he can say a word, Bill, quarterback of the local school's team, turns, smiles, and greets him, "Joe, good to see you. Want some pizza?" Bill asks Joe how he's doing and actually shows a genuine interest in him.

Joe confesses, "I'm having a hard time getting used to high school, especially my algebra class."

Bill responds, "I'm terrible at math, but Tom over there is a genius." Bill calls Tom over. Joe marvels at these two as they joke around and hug each other. Bill is clean cut and nicely dressed. Tom has ripped jeans, orange hair, a tattoo, and a nose ring. These guys can't be friends, Joe thinks to himself. Bill tells Tom about Joe's math woes.

Tom meets Joe and asks, "Do you want some help? I'm a math tutor."

Joe is dumbstruck. "Sure," he says.

As he walks into the meeting area with Tom, Sally hands him a program and says, "Hey, a bunch of us are playing broomball afterwards, do you want to come?" As Joe sits down, he is awed how different these people are.

What would your life be like if all the people around you made it their entire goal to be a blessing to you? What kind of difference would that make in your life? This is the difference that God is calling you to make in the lives of others as you live out His plans for your life.

The difference is WHATEVER. The example above is about Christians who know and live out God's purpose for their relationships: to serve others. How? Using WHATEVER gift God has given. Why? So that in all things God may be praised. Are your relationships glorifying God because of the way you are serving others using whatever it takes? God's purpose for your relationships is that you bless others. Did you ever think if it that way before?

Sibling or spouse?
The problem gets worse when see others through a lens that views them as potential mates or worse, as sexual objects, instead of as brothers or sisters. This personal potential view is based on the rejection of others in the pursuit of Mr. or Ms. Right.

How do you know if you have this perspective? When you walk into a group of people, what are some of the first things that come

"Do not rebuke an older man harshly, but exhort him as if he were your father. Treat younger men as brothers, older women as mothers, and younger women as sisters, with absolute purity."
1 Timothy 5:1,2

to mind? Think of the first words you say inside your head. Do you use words (not out loud, of course, because everyone would think that you are unspiritual) such as cute, pretty, babe, she's hot, or ugly, fat, nasty, dork, loser? Do you avoid or pursue people based on their looks, popularity, or personality? These are indicators that you view people not as God views them but as the world views them.

YCAMITNI?

NO it's not the latest Mexican rave. It's intimacy spelled *backwards*. Too often our *relationships* make about as much sense as ycamitni, because we also get them upside down and backwards. This happens when we *view* others as potential mates. That perspective turns upside down the priorities our relationships should have. How? By treating everyone as a potential mate, we attach sexual significance to every relationship. We make every relationship sexual. You may be saying, "No way, you've crossed the line this time." Let's look at same sex relationships. If you walked by two guys giving each other a hug in the hall what would you think? What would most of the people in your school think? You know what I'm talking about. Just fill in the blank. Look at those guys, they're _____!

Upset is the word you chose, right? Well, maybe not. But what if I told you that the mother of the two brothers had cancer and that one of them was upset? You might say, "Well I didn't know." But that's just the point, you *probably* reacted to their physical contact as being sexual. This super-charged sexual atmosphere that permeates our culture actually works against intimacy, especially for guys. The idea of showing any form of affection is viewed as homosexual. So guys just don't show affection for each other or they worry inappropriately about their sexual orientation because there are no other choices available to them.

When we view others primarily as potential mates and when we see caring physical contact in relationships as sexual, we miss out on real intimacy. Part of the reason for this distorted view is that we don't understand that there are various forms of physical contact. Let's look at three levels of physical touch.

1. Social intimacy.

    This type of contact is represented in the way that we greet someone who we are meeting in a social situation. In the United States, we shake hands. Hand shaking is a socially accepted and expected form of contact. In fact, not to do so could be viewed as a sign of disrespect. Other examples of social physical contact might be seen in a game or job in which contact is necessary. An example of this might be tagging a player out in a baseball game.

> *We miss out on real imtimacy.*

2. Emotional intimacy.

This form of contact conveys messages of love and care for each other. Examples of this include holding a crying child, kissing your mother, holding hands with someone in prayer, patting your teammate on the back after he scores a goal, hugging a good friend. You get the idea. The list goes on and on. This type of contact communicates strong emotional content that is appropriately shared in many types of relationships. This type of physical contact, however, can be negative as well as positive. For example one person might angrily shove another in a football game. However, by and large, this is the kind of contact that brothers and sisters engage in to encourage, build up, express care, and personal support.

3. Sexual intimacy.

This form of contact conveys messages that contain sexual content. This, as we mentioned earlier, is what intercourse means. It means communication or commerce. So sexual intercourse is sexual communication with another person. This means that intercourse can occur even without physical contact. People can communicate sexual messages apart from ever touching each other. However, for our purposes here, we are talking about physical contact that is designed to stimulate a sexual response.

As we will see in the next section entitled God's Way, God created our sexual nature, called it good, and then declared that marriage is the only arena where it is to be expressed. God wants us to experience love and acceptance from our family and friendships. He wants us to understand that physical affection is a healthy part of those relationships. Physical affection is always good in appropriate relationships, but sexual expression is a unique and powerful gift reserved only for marriage.

Are your relationships upside down and backwards?

Intimacy right side up.
Intimacy gets lost when we put on a front trying to impress others. This mentality comes in part from the conveyer belt of performance model. We are afraid that if anyone really knew us, they would reject us. That's why God wants us to have the security of brother-sister relationships. Acting smooth is laughable in these relationships. We don't dress up for our siblings, or act differently than who we really are, even though there may be times when putting forth more effort with our brothers and sisters is exactly what we should do. When done properly, we should be able to enjoy the anxiety-free closeness that brothers and sisters in Christ can and should have. Talking together, sharing feelings, and engaging in activities like bowling and basketball are all things that we can enjoy with one another. A pat on the back, an arm around the shoulder, and a hug are all components of positive and appropriate physical intimacy between siblings. But a guy would never kiss his sister or think about having sex with her. It goes against the way that God created us.

Practice makes imperfect

"How do you get really good at the guitar, Dad?" my son asked me. "Alex you need to practice a lot — practice makes perfect!" I quoted him this old proverb to teach him how to improve at a skill he desired. But that same principle applies to skills and lifestyles we don't desire as well. In these cases, practice makes us imperfect. If we allow the wrong behaviors and values to infiltrate our lives, we find that they become habits and those habits, practiced over and over, take us farther and farther away from the perfection that God envisions for our lives. So we do need to practice, but we need to practice intimacy and physical expressions of such intimacies within the boundaries that God has defined.

Breaking up is hard to do -- NOT!

An old song by Neil Sedaka says that "Breaking up is hard to do," but let's face it — it's not! When we practice this world's method of relationships, we practice breaking up. In fact, we practice divorce! Then we wonder how we, as members of the Church, became so good at it.

Did you know physical contact can be negative or positive?

Let me explain. Boy meets girl. Boy likes girl. Boy and girl make an inappropriate vow like, "Let's be boyfriend and girlfriend." Boy gets tired of girl. He likes a new girl. Like a script from a bad movie, he recites the lines, "Jenny I really like you a lot, but…" He "breaks up" with girl, and now is "going out" with the new girl. Sound familiar?

No division adds up.

Here's where the world's way of relationships goes wrong. First, the Bible teaches that brothers and sisters don't break up -- ever! Belonging, acceptance, and unity are what the family of God is all about. *"Make every effort to keep the unity of the Spirit through the bond of peace. There is one body and one Spirit--just as you were called to one hope when you were called-- one Lord, one faith, one baptism; one God and Father of all, who is over all and through all and in all"* (Ephesians 4:3-6). In case we missed the call to unity and peace, take note that this passage uses the word *one* seven times!

God wants his people to be one. He doesn't want us dividing up over every little thing. *"There should be no division in the body, but that its parts should have equal concern for each other"* (1 Corinthians 12:25). How many youth group romances have brought division, destruction, and bitterness to people? There is no contraceptive for a broken heart. Our unity is also a strong witness to the world. Jesus prayed that we would be *"brought to complete unity to let the world know that you sent me and have loved them even as you have loved me"* (John 17:23). Does this convince you that God's way of relationships is radically different than the world's way? It should. We need to be hearers and doers of God's Word. The Word of God is not like a resale shop where we try on what we like and leave the rest behind. All of God's Word is true. All of His commands are to be followed and obeyed.

Let's say that an individual has 12 years of dating before they begin to date Mr. or Ms. Right. How many people have they included in these dating relationships? For illustration purposes, let's say 21, and this last person is the person they are going to marry. What do you think are their chances of having a strong and fulfilling marriage? That person has gone out with and divorced/broken up with 20 people! How many have they committed to and stayed with for a lifetime - none! This person has practiced divorce his/her entire relationship life. When things get hard, what do you think a person with that track record is going to do?

Lower self-esteem guaranteed!

And talk about self-esteem! When we view members the opposite sex as potential mates, we are wrong every time except once. At best, only one will ever be your spouse. How would you feel if you got every answer on every test in every class wrong every time except once? What would your grade be? In the school of life, you can study hard and fail the test. Why? Because we are studying from the wrong book! Melrose Place, Rolling Stone, and the WB are not going to teach you what you need to know to pass the test of good relationships, but God's Word will. God's Word tells us that if you treat everyone as a brother or sister and you eventually get married, then you are right every time!

God doesn't want to help you be better at the world's conveyer belt method of relationships where every encounter is a new chance to be rejected. God's whole goal for His children is to get them off the conveyer belt of performance. Experiencing love and acceptance by Him and His people is what He desires for you. But to really experience this to the fullest, we need a new view of relationships. We need to see people and relationships through God's eyes. Relationships that bless others, using whatever gifts He has given us, come from the heart of God. He wants us to see each connection with others as an opportunity to love and serve, bringing glory to Him. God loves you. He knows what's best for you. He has the power to bring it about. His way is the best way. Let's focus on that.

We need a new view of relationships.

Dig Deeper: God's View

*"...and that in this matter no one should wrong his brother or take advantage of him. The Lord will punish men for all such sins, as we have already told you and warned you" (*I Thessalonians 4:6).

*"This, then, is how you should pray: <u>Our Father</u> in heaven, hallowed be your name," (*Matthew 6:9 emphasis added).

According to I Timothy 5:1-2, John 1:12, and Ephesians 3:14-15, what does God teach about how to view our relationships with Himself and with one another?

In Matthew 22:37-40, what is the type of relationship that God wants us to have with Himself and with others?

Where's The Love?

"Now about brotherly love..." (1 Thessalonians 4:9).

God's purpose in relationships is to bless others.

"Each one should use whatever gift he has received to serve others... so that in all things God may be praised through Jesus Christ. To him be the glory and the power for ever and ever." Amen
(I Peter 4:10-11).

Read also Philippians 2:3-8 and I Peter 4:7-11.

From these verses, what do you conclude our goal should be in our relationships?

Make a list of all the ways that brother/sister relationships differ from boyfriend/girlfriend relationships.

God _____ you. He knows what's _____ for you. He has the _____ to bring it about. Then the best way is...

> *"There should be no division in the body, but that its parts should have equal concern for each other."*
>
> *1 Corinthians 12:25*

Journal Page

Take Action

Pray asking God to identify a statement and/or scripture that was meaningful to you in this chapter.

On your journal page, write this statement or scripture passage as well as any other thoughts or feelings you have in response to what you are learning.

Know God's View

Memory Verses

"...and that in this matter no one should wrong his brother or take advantage of him. The Lord will punish men for all such sins, as we have already told you and warned you," (1 Thessalonians 4:6).

"This, then, is how you should pray: Our Father in heaven, hallowed be your name," (Matthew 6:9 emphasis added).

Read John 1:12 and Ephesians 3:14-15.

According to Matthew 6:9, what is the relational word that Jesus tells us to use of God?

What is the word used to describe other believers in 1 Thessalonians 4:6?

What does God teach us about how to view our relationships with Him and with one another?

According to all these verses, our primary relationship to God is not

> Employer/Employee
> Teacher/Student
> Agent/Client
> Master/Slave
> Creator/Creation

Our Father teaches us that the foundation of all our relationships is family. When we enter into His Family through His Son, Jesus, we become children of God. As His children, we now have a multitude of brothers and sisters. How does God want us to treat our brothers and sisters?

Know God's View

Read I Timothy 5:1-2 and Philippians 2:3-8.

What does it mean to treat younger women as sisters with absolute purity?

When you see someone else, do you see them as a brother/sister or as a potential mate/boyfriend/girlfriend?

One of the ways that we are often conformed to this world is that we see others through a lens that views them as potential mates or worse, as sexual objects. What are some of the problems with this way of viewing others?

Based on the verses above and others that you have read, is this a biblical view? Why or why not?

One significant way that this view has problems, aside from sexual immorality, is that it is based on the rejection of others in the pursuit of Mr. or Ms. Right. How do you know if you have this perspective? When you walk into a group of people, what are some of the first things that come to mind?

Please make a list of words that the people you know or hang out with might use.

Day by Day

Day 2

Do you make decisions to avoid or pursue relationships with others based on your view of their looks, popularity, or personality? These are indicators that you view people not as God views them, but as the world views them.

Another problem with viewing others as potential mates is that it turns upside down the priorities our relationships should have. Rather than receiving all people and appreciating them for who they are, we reject them. We move away from love and hasten toward lust. We give up meaningful relationships that look to the real person inside, made in the very image of God and instead settle for a small world of acquaintances. God, in His wisdom, knows this. This attitude wrecks our potential for real intimacy, where we can give and receive love that isn't tainted by mixed motives. The reason this attitude wrecks our relationships is that it is based on self-centered lust rather than God-centered love.

How well are you doing in the area of viewing people as brothers/sisters first?

Where do you need to improve in this area?

God desires that we would view each other as family.

Know God's View

Read Ephesians 3:14-21, Matthew 7:11, Matthew 22:37-40, and 1 John 4:16. (optional additional reading could include John 3:16, Isaiah 43:4, and Isaiah 64:8)

After reading these passages, how do you think God views you?

Does your heavenly Father love you? How do you know?

After reading Matthew 7:11, describe the kinds of gifts the heavenly Father gives His children.

In 1-2 sentences, describe your relationship with God.

According to Matthew 22:37-40, what is the **type** of relationship were you created to have with God?

Is that the type of relationship that you have now?

Describe what a love relationship with God would look like.

How would such a relationship affect a normal day in your life? Be specific.

Other optional questions:

How would you describe your relationship with your earthly father and family?

What is one thing that you could do to improve those family relationships?
Pray that God would help you to love your family as you love yourself.

Day by Day

Day 3

Know God's View

Read Matthew 22:37-40, Philippians 2:3-8, 1 Peter 4:7-11, and 1 Thessalonians 4:9.

What type of relationship does God want you to have with others?

Day by Day

Day 4

Based on I Peter 4:10-11, what should be our goal in our relationships?

Verse 11 of I Peter 4 ends with a key phrase regarding the purpose of our relationships, *so that in all things* (the ways we serve and minister to others) *God may be praised through Jesus Christ.* Is God praised in the way you relate to others, especially members of the opposite sex?

How?

In what ways do you need to consider others more highly than yourself, as Philippians 2:3 shows?

Know God's View

Read I Corinthians 13:1-8.

Make a list of all the ways that brother/sister relationships differ from boyfriend/girlfriend relationships.

Rate yourself on a scale of (1 - terrible and 10 - excellent) on the characteristics given below. In my relationships with others (parents, family, friends, member of the opposite sex) I am ...

patient   _____

kind   _____

not envious   _____

not boastful   _____

not proud   _____

not self-seeking   _____

not easily angered   _____

keeping no record of wrongs   _____

not delighting in evil   _____

rejoicing with the truth   _____

protective of others   _____

trusting of others   _____

hoping the best for others   _____

persevering with others   _____

unfailing   _____

Day by Day

Day 5

Go back over this list now and describe what these things might look like in your behavior in relationships. (e.g. **Patient—5:** "I have been pressuring my girlfriend to do things that she doesn't want to do. If I love her, I will recognize that this is wrong and self-seeking. I will treat her like a sister with honor and will not pressure her. I will **wait** until marriage for sexual intimacy."

Return to the list of love characteristics above. God is love and God loves you. Read the list one more time, except begin with **"Because God loves me He is patient with me..."** Believe it or not it's true this is how God feels about you. Pray that God would help you to experience His love more fully and to help you show His love to others.

God loves you.

He knows what is best for you.

He has the power to bring it about.

The best way is always GOD'S WAY!

God is love

and

God loves

you.

Know God's View

Review and reflect.

Review the verse for the week and all five previous days of devotions.

What are the three biggest lessons you learned from this week's materials?

For each of those lessons, write a one-sentence statement explaining why it impressed you.

How does this material relate to staying pure and holy?

Day by Day

Day 6

CHAPTER 4   KNOW GOD'S WAY

Truth or consequences.

If many of us are honest, we have to admit that there have been times when we question God's wisdom, goodness, and love. For example the Lord gave us these bodies complete with physical/sexual desires, didn't He?

Then we are told to control them.

We sometimes wonder if God isn't really a celestial killjoy out to...

> Steal our pleasure
> Kill our excitement
> Destroy our lives

And this is exactly where Satan wants us to think!

If you think any of the above things, you are calling God a liar! In fact, you are attributing the characteristics of Satan to God! Jesus explains the difference when He says, *"The thief comes only to steal and kill and destroy; I have come that they may have life, and have it to the full"* (John 10:10).

Satan is the Father of lies. The method that he uses today is the same one that he has used from the beginning of time. In fact, we find he set up the very first sin on this earth by lying and creating doubt about the true loving nature of God.

"Now the serpent was more crafty than any of the wild animals the LORD God had made. He said to the woman, "Did God really say, 'You must not eat from any tree in the garden'" (Genesis 3:1)?

That question, which planted the seed of doubt in Eve's mind, led to the first sin. Her sinful decision is affecting you right now! One of the lies that Satan has probably used on you is "Did God really say, `You must not _____(fill in the blank here)?"

Do you see how Satan plants doubt and causes you to make rationalizations for behavior that you want to be able to do and still call yourself a Christian? Believing that liar will only bring ruin and disaster to your life, especially in the area of your sexuality. That's why the Bible says, *"Flee from sexual immorality. All other sins a man commits are outside his body, but he who sins sexually sins against his own body"* (I Corinthians 6:18). If you have believed the lies of Satan, you can confess that to the Lord right now and then move toward truth, freedom, and life. Jesus said *"I have come that you might have life and have it to the full"* (John 10:10). That's the truth, don't settle for the consequences of believing a lie.

Think positively.

Free association is process that communicates our immediate, top-of-the-head thoughts and attitudes about certain topics. Using that technique, free associate your answer to this question: What do you think of when you think of Christianity and sexuality?

Many times participants in our seminars respond with words such as *evil, bad, don't,* and *sin.* Unfortunately, many of our Christian young people have been taught this negative view of sexuality. The problem, though, is that this view is not only negative, it's unbiblical! The Bible teaches that sex is fulfilling, relational, loving, and rewarding **when** it is confined within the marriage boundaries that God has set up. Free associations about sex should be positive, not negative, if we are following what the Bible teaches.

Don't get burned.

Why would God give us something so good and so tempting and then tell us to control it?

"Can a man scoop fire into his lap without his clothes being burned" (Proverbs 6:27)?

Imagine with me that you and a friend are hiking in the snow-covered peaks of Colorado. There's not another soul or house for miles around. It's a beautiful, but very cold, day. Finally you reach the snow covered cabin that has been your day-long destination. It's a rustic cabin with no heat. You are looking forward to getting warm and having a nice warm meal. All you need now is a fire. A fire in a fireplace would be a wonderful thing, a powerful thing, a warm thing. Yes. You appreciate the beautiful stone fireplace before you. You already imagine it providing needed heat for your body and a heat source over which to cook your dinner. The radiating fireplace will be comfortable and pleasant to be around.

Your attention is shockingly broken by the first crackle and pop of flame licking wood. You realize, with alarm, that your friend has already started to build the fire, but he is building it in the middle of the room against the main wooden support beam of the cabin.

"What are you doing? Are you out of your mind?" you say.

His reply takes you by surprise, "You always think you know best, don't you? Why don't you mind your own business."

"Bill, I'm not trying to offend you, but you are going to kill us, and burn your folks' cabin down. Why don't we move the fire to the fireplace?"

God created

sex, therefore

it is good ...

very good.

"No. I'm freezing and I want to eat now."

You watch the flames begin to hungrily devour the dry post, and think, "This can't be happening to me." As you struggle with whether to try to put the fire out or run out of the cabin into the cold darkness, you wake with a start.

Crazy nightmare, you say. But you may be experiencing that kind of insanity right now. If you are not, I guarantee that someone around you is. You see, our sexuality is just like a fire. Inside the boundaries that God has set up, His fireplace of marriage, it is a wonderful gift. He created sexual union for married couples as a source of joy and as an expression of love. In fact, God exalted this act of intimacy by making it the means through which He blesses couples with children.

But if we take our sexuality out of the fireplace, the boundaries that God has set, and burn it wherever we want, it is a dangerous thing. Outside of the protective boundaries of marriage, sex destroys. Everyone gets burned. It burns down dreams and destroys lives. God isn't trying to ruin your life with the rules He set up. He's trying to save it.

Burn the fire in the fireplace.
"There is a way that seems right to a man but in the end it leads to death" (Proverbs 14:12).

On the other hand, God, the Master Designer, has a positive plan for sexuality and relationships. Let's read about it in Genesis.

"The LORD God said, "It is not good for the man to be alone. I will make a helper suitable for him. Now the LORD God had formed out of the ground all the beasts of the field and all the birds of the air. He brought them to the man to see what he would name them; and whatever the man called each living creature, that was its name. So the man gave names to all the livestock, the birds of the air and all the beasts of the field. But for Adam no suitable helper was found. So the LORD God caused the man to fall into a deep sleep; and while he was sleeping, he took one of the man's ribs and closed up the place with flesh. Then the LORD God made a woman from the rib he had taken out of the man, and he brought her to the man. The man said, "This is now bone of my bones and flesh of my flesh; she shall be called `woman', for she was taken out of man." For this reason a man will leave his father and mother and be united to his wife, and they will become one flesh. The man and his wife were both naked, and they felt no shame (Genesis 2:18-25).

Let's look at what God tells us about intimate relationships in this passage.

God created sex to be used within the boundaries of marriage.

Not Good, Definitely Not Good.

The LORD God said, *"It is not good for the man to be alone. I will make a helper suitable for him"* (Genesis 2:18).

When God created the earth, He looked at all that He created and announced that it was "good." The first situation mentioned in the Bible as being "not good" is that man was alone. It is important to note that this observation of the aloneness of man was before the fall. This desire for relationship with others is not the result of sin. It is the result of the way God intentionally created us. Relationships are his idea. It is important to see here, as well, that God recognized the need and formulated the solution before the man could even mouth the request.

Help Wanted.

"Now the LORD God had formed out of the ground all the beasts of the field and all the birds of the air. He brought them to the man to see what he would name them; and whatever the man called each living creature, that was its name. So the man gave names to all the livestock, the birds of the air and all the beasts of the field. But for Adam no suitable helper was found" (Genesis 2:19-20).

God allows for and encourages creativity in our lives. You can almost see the smile on God's face as he brings the animals to Adam to see what he would name them. An important part of this passage is that as God brings new activity into Adam's life, He does not forget Adam's lack of companionship. He doesn't forget yours either. However, His timing is always perfect. God wants Adam to properly appreciate the gift he is going to receive, for her sake, for Adam's sake, and for God's glory. So the gift had to be given in God's perfect time.

Recently, my daughter was tugging on my leg crying for a "nana" (that's baby talk for banana). I picked her up and held her as she cried all the louder because the fruit bowl was now in sight. I told her "No, honey it's not ripe yet." As the wailing reached its ultimate crescendo, I decided to give her what she was pleading for. As we began peeling the green banana, you could see the protective peel straining against being opened and the stringy innards still clinging to the fruit. I scraped this off and offered her a bite. She bit the fruit and a look of realization came over her face; her expression turned from confusion to disgust. She promptly spit the unripened fruit out of her mouth and it hit the floor with a splat. She then looked at me as though I had betrayed her and cried for me to take the fruit back.

It's not that the fruit was bad, it just wasn't ripe yet. If it is eaten prematurely, the taste is not nearly as good as it was intended to be. The fruit that was meant to bring pleasure and nourishment ended up being scorned and discarded.

> *"It is not good for man to be alone."*
>
> **Genesis 2:18**

That incident caused me to wonder about how often we do this with God in general but especially in our relationships. We mistake mercy for meanness, protection for punishment, love for lies, faithfulness for forgetfulness. God is a merciful, protective, loving, and faithful father. He wants us to appreciate His good gifts in all their fullness. Let it be the ripe time. His time.

The verse ends with God's remembrance *"But for Adam no suitable helper was found"* (Genesis 2:20). God didn't forget Adam and He won't forget you.

<u>The Great Provider.</u>

So the Lord God caused the man to fall into a deep sleep; and while he was sleeping, he took one of the man's ribs and closed up the place with flesh. Then the LORD God made a woman from the rib he had taken out of the man, and he brought her to the man. The man said, 'This is now bone of my bones and flesh of my flesh; she shall be called `woman', for she was taken out of man'" (Genesis 2:22-23).

God made a helper suitable for Adam. He can make one for you too! Made for each other. Made from each other. I often say that my wife is my better half. I know some people, when they hear that, will argue, "You're not half a person. You are whole in Christ." I would agree, sort of.

We live in the United States where we worship independence. We even named a national holiday in its honor. But personal independence is not what God intended. He created us for relationship and for dependence on one another. I believe this is one of the reasons that we do relationships so poorly. Many of the young people I speak with ask me, "Why am I so lonely even though I am seldom alone?" God has a bigger plan for you than loneliness and a better plan than independence.

God created a partner for Adam, He can provide one for us also.

In God's creation of this plan for relationship, we can see three critical factors. They are

- Vulnerability
- Offering
- Reception

<u>Vulnerability</u>

Adam goes to sleep. In his sleep, he becomes vulnerable, and God literally opens him up. He's like a lot of us. We want to be open, but often it only happens because God takes the initiative. It's also interesting to note that God took from Adam's side a rib. The ribs have an important job and that job is to protect the heart. God wants us to guard our hearts but if we are ever going to connect at a heart level with others, we need to take some risks and let go of some of our defenses.

Offering

God took one of Adam's ribs. It is interesting to see here that God didn't make another person from dust. He could have. He chose to take a piece of Adam to make Eve. Interesting. I believe God wanted to make a point. We have to give of ourselves to make a relationship happen. It has to cost us something, otherwise the relationship lacks value to us.

Reception

Adam receives the gift that God gives him in Eve with great joy. In fact, the most poetic praise that Adam ever utters is offered up at this time. We need to receive the good gifts that God brings us in our relationships, especially in our relationship with Him. The God who provided for Adam will provide for you, too. He's the same God. How did Adam find his wife? He didn't find her, even though he searched. God brought her to Adam in His perfect timing. Go to sleep and trust the Father to provide.

Of sexuality and starfish.
"For this reason a man will leave his father and mother and be united to his wife, and they will become one flesh" (Genesis 2:24).

I can remember it vividly. I was with family and friends at Jones Beach. Looking out at the Atlantic Ocean on a warm sunny morning and tasting the salt air, I was about to learn a lesson about sexuality. My friend came up to me with an excited smile and said, "I want to show you something really cool under the boardwalk over there."

"Okay, I said," wondering what this cool discovery would be. As we got there I said, as only an eight-year-old can, "Whoa." The entire place was filled with starfish.

My friend said, "Watch this," as he plucked one of them off the cement wall. He then proceeded to pull the starfish's arm off.

Disgusted, I asked "What are you doing?"

"Don't worry," he assured me, "they grow them back".

God could have made you like an amoeba or starfish. Certain varieties of these organisms are asexual. Simply put, asexual beings reproduce individually by dividing. They don't need partners. They don't need relationships. They have independence down pat. God could have made you and me this way, too, but He didn't. Why? Because sexuality is His idea. He created it and called it good. We need to agree with God. Sexual intimacy is God's plan, not Satan's. There is nothing creative about Satan. He can only pervert the good things that God has created.

> *God could have made you as an amoeba or starfish.*

Relationships, intimacy and sexuality are all God's ideas! What a great inventor!

The best lover.
"For this reason a man will leave his father and mother and be united to his wife, and they will become one flesh." (Genesis 2:24).

By now you know a lot more about God's way than you may have known before you started this book, but the best is yet to come. I don't know what you are good at. Maybe you're the best tuba player in your town. What I do know is that there are probably several things that you are not good at. We live in a culture that often assigns worth based on performance. "He's the best," "She's awesome," "I'd love to be in his shoes," are statements that can often be heard regarding basketball players, singers, and CEO's. God wants to free us from measuring ourselves in this way and from basing our worth on comparisons. He definitely wants to free us from this kind of comparison in our intimate relationships.

Think with me for one minute. Imagine God has brought you a wonderful woman and you are married. If you have never had sex and neither has your wife, then who is the best lover you are ever going to have? **Your wife**. Who is the best lover that your wife is ever going to have? **You**! This is not a trick question. This it what God intended for you from the beginning. He planned for you to be unique and special for your spouse in every way. He planned that in marriage you would share something that completely belongs only to the two of you.

God desires for you to experience trust, intimacy, faithfulness, and wholeness instead of the broken relationships, broken lives, and broken hearts that the world has to offer. As one person has said, "There is no contraceptive for a broken heart." He made you as a unique creation, special in his sight, and He desires to give you the best. He desires for you to experience the great value and worth with which He sees you.

God wants you to be the best! Don't settle for less.

"Do you not know that your body is a temple of the Holy Spirit, who is in you, whom you have received from God? You are not your own; you were bought at a price. Therefore honor God with your body" (1 Corinthians 6:19-20).

You are created in the image of the living God and have been bought with a great price. He wants you to be the best! Don't steal this blessing from yourself!

Pass the test.
In what relationship do all these blessing come? God says that you are to be united to:

Anyone
My friend
My fiancée
My spouse

Too many people get the wrong answer on this test and end up flunking out of their relationships. God wants you to pass the test and He is prejudiced…in your favor! He, in fact, let's you take this test as an open book exam. So open the book!

"Examine yourselves to see whether you are in the faith; test yourselves. Do you not realize that Christ Jesus is in you-- unless, of course, you fail the test" (2 Corinthians 13:5)?

There is a group of people that I encounter who have to take a second test. You see, these people often tell me that God isn't making up a bunch of rules. They choose to believe that they are saved and, therefore, they can live as they want to live. When I hear that argument, I ask them a very simple question: "If you're living like hell what makes you think you're going to heaven?"

Taken aback they often reply, "Well, I prayed and asked Jesus into my heart."

"Why?"

"Well, my parents told me I should?"

"Why?"

"Because I don't want to go to hell?"

"Why?"

"Because it's a real bad place and God isn't there."

"You mean like your life is now?"

"Yeah, I guess so."

What I have to tell this person and anyone else who doesn't want to follow the instructions God gives for living is this. If you don't want God in your life now, what makes you think you're going to want Him later? You may have asked Jesus into your life to take away your sins, but did you really mean it? God doesn't just listen to your words, He listens to your heart. *"These people honor me with their lips, but their hearts are far from me"* (Matthew 15:8).

Do you want Jesus to take your sin away? Really*? "But you know that he appeared so that he might take away our sins"* (I John 3:5). He will do it, if you want Him to. When He comes into a life, He changes it, but only as much as you'll let Him. This doesn't mean that you will be perfect, but it does mean that you receive Him into your life and you allow Him to take control.

"Yet to all who received him, to those who believed in his name, he gave the right to become children of God" (John 1:12).

"Therefore, if anyone is in Christ, he is a new creation; the old has gone, the new has come" (II Corinthians 5:17)!

Sex for dummies.
"For this reason a man will leave his father and mother and be united to his wife, and they will become one flesh. The man and his wife were both naked, and they felt no shame" (Genesis 2:24-25).

The Bible says, *"My people are destroyed from lack of knowledge."* (Hosea 4:6). That's a pretty simple statement, and it certainly applies to the topic of purity and holiness. One reason many people have encountered great personal destruction in the area of relationships is due to a lack of knowledge and understanding of sexual intimacy. Intimacy is much more than sexuality! Don't settle for sex without intimacy. Don't settle for less than what God has to offer!

The Bible uses the words *to know* as a term for intimacy because it is the Creator's intent that husbands and wives wouldn't just have sex, but that they would *know* each other. *"And Adam <u>knew</u> Eve his wife; and she conceived,"* (Genesis 4:1 emphasis added).

Isn't that awesome? Do you want the person you love to have sex with you or to *know* you? What does it mean to know someone at the depth implied by that biblical term? I liken this kind of knowing to the sacraments of Communion or Baptism. Is Communion just eating a bagel and juice? Is Baptism just a public bathing experience? In both cases, the answer is "No." Both Communion and Baptism are outward expressions of an inward reality. Let me illustrate this concept using Communion as an example.

For I received from the Lord what I also passed on to you: The Lord Jesus, on the night he was betrayed, took bread, and when he had given thanks, he broke it and said, 'This is my body, which is for you; do this in remembrance of me.' In the same way, after supper he took the cup, saying, 'This cup is the new covenant in my blood; do this, whenever you drink it, in remembrance of me.' For whenever you eat this bread and drink this cup, you proclaim the Lord's death until he comes. Therefore, whoever eats the bread or drinks the cup of the Lord in an unworthy manner will be guilty of sinning against the body and blood of the Lord (1 Corinthians 11:23-27).

Communion is a spiritual, emotional, physical, and relational experience. Spiritually, you remember the Lord and affirm the new life He has given you as a child of God. Emotionally, you rejoice in this truth, with thankfulness in your heart, warmed by the love God

Sex is more than a physical act!

has shown you and the love in which you are growing towards Him. Physically, you eat the bread and drink the cup. Relationally, you do this with other brothers and sisters affirming your common beliefs and proclaiming to the world the Lord's death and resurrection. Do you see how much more this is than just a physical act? We need to view the truth about our sexuality in the same way.

Sexual intimacy is a lot like your relationship with Jesus. It's personal in these ways:

- Physical intimacy
- Emotional intimacy
- Relational intimacy
- Spiritual intimacy
- Obedience to God's Plan
- Nourishment for the whole being
- Acknowledgment by God, others, and yourself
- Expression of love

You honor your spouse by acknowledging the relationship before God and man through marriage.

Let me build this example from the bottom up. As you come to know your spouse, you love him or her and, in doing so, you will do everything in your power to honor your lover. *"I tell you the truth, the man who does not enter the sheep pen by the gate, but climbs in by some other way, is a thief and a robber"* (John 10:1). A good friend of mine, Bob Hoey, likes to use the passage above as an example of the marriage covenant. Thieves come in covertly. The man of honor comes in through the front door. You honor your spouse by acknowledging the relationship before God and man through marriage. Your goal in this relationship is to serve your spouse, nourishing your relationship. You desire for this relationship to grow. You do all of these things in obedience to God, knowing that His way is the best way. Spiritually, you begin to experience the oneness that God intended. You come to know firsthand that, as Ecclesiastes tells us, a cord of three strands is not easily broken. You have strength together as you encourage one another, pray together, serve together, grow in maturity together, and as you forgive and love one another in greater and greater degrees.

Your relationship moves to new depths as you experience emotional strength, support, and vulnerability through and with one another. This foundation finds its fulfillment and completion in physical oneness which is the outward expression of a very deep and satisfying inward reality. This is the kind of fulfilling relationship that God desires for you, not a cheap and shallow counterfeit. And there's more! When your love life with your spouse is this close, then you experience this next truth.

No shame no game.
"The man and his wife were both naked, and they felt no shame" (Genesis 2:25).

Man and wife. The benefits of what we are discussing here are intended to be an exclusive benefit of husbands and wives. God's design was that the husband and wife would be naked and unashamed. Imagine for a moment that you have just shared some of your greatest hopes and fears with your spouse. You are open and transparent and have put up no front. You are real. And you know **no shame**! I know people who would pay big dollars for this experience: The opportunity to find one real friend. Someone who is faithful and who cares.

"... *there is a friend who sticks closer than a brother*" (Proverbs 18:24). Jesus is that friend. And yet He desires that we should experience this kind of relationship in parts of His creation as well as with Him. Marriage is one such place. This is the very reason that marriage is used as an example of Christ's relationship with the Church, His bride.

"*For this reason a man will leave his father and mother and be united to his wife, and the two will become one flesh.*" *This is a profound mystery--but I am talking about Christ and the church. However, each one of you also must love his wife as he loves himself, and the wife must respect her husband*" (Ephesians 5:31-33). God created marriage to be a source of closeness beyond what we can understand, but not beyond what we can experience.

You were made by God, not to be used and abused, but to be honored and cherished in a committed, connected, and growing relationship. That relationship is first and foremost with Him and then with your God-given spouse. Don't settle for less.

You were made by God, not to be used and abused!

Dig Deeper: God's Way

"For God did not call us to be impure, but to live a holy life." (1 Thessalonians 4:7).

"As for God, his way is perfect;" (II Samuel 22:31).

List verses given in this chapter and other that you can find that support our need to acknowledge and follow God's way.

As for God,

His way is

perfect.

II Samuel 22:31

KNOW GOD'S POSITIVE PLAN FOR HIS PEOPLE.

Read Genesis 2:18-25.

What does this passage tell you about God's plan for intimate relationships?

"Whoever has my commands and obeys them, he is the one who loves me. He who loves me will be loved by my Father, and I too will love him and show myself to him" (John 14:21).

You have his commands. You know his will. Do you love Him...really? If you do, then you will obey Him. To obey Him, what will you need to do in the areas of purity and holiness?

Journal Page

Take Action

Pray asking God to identify a statement and/or scripture that was meaningful to you in this chapter.

On your journal page, write this statement or scripture passage as well as any other thoughts or feelings you have in response to what you are learning.

God's Way

Memory Verses
"For God did not call us to be impure, but to live a holy life." (1 Thessalonians 4:7).

"As for God his way is perfect;" (II Samuel 22:31).

Day by Day

Day 1

Read John 10:10, Genesis 2:18 and 20b-25.

List the first three words that come to mind when you think of Christianity and sexuality.

When you think of your sexuality, do you see God as bringing blessing to your life, or do you see Him as a thief who wants to steal pleasure, kill excitement, and destroy life? Why?

In the Genesis passage, what does the Lord call "not good"?

Is this comment made before man's fall into sin or after?

How did Adam find his wife?

Who provided a helper suitable for Adam?

If you follow the Lord and it's His will for you to be married, who will provide a helper suitable for you?

How can you live this belief out?

What is Adam going to sleep a sign of?

How do you need to "go to sleep" in terms of seeking an intimate relationship?

God's Way

Read Genesis 2:18 and 20b-25.

Who invented intimacy and sexuality?

What did God call his creation according to Genesis 1:31?

Okay? Fair? Good? VERY GOOD! And so should we! Intimacy and sexuality are God's idea--He invented them. Yeah, God!!

Who is the man united to according to these scriptures?

Intimacy is much more than sexuality. It is a spiritual, emotional, and physical union. It is intended to be a holy expression of covenant love in marriage. With this in mind, what do you think the statement that they were "naked and unashamed" means . . .

. . .spiritually?

. . .emotionally?

. . .physically?

Go back to the first two questions on Day 1. Is your view of God and Christianity in line with what the Bible says about sexuality? Explain.

Look again at II Samuel 22:31. The word of the Lord is FLAWLESS! Agree with this --Then follow what God says in His Word.!

God's Way is the BEST WAY.

Day by Day

Day 2

God's Way

Keep the fire in the fireplace.

Read II Samuel 22:31 and Proverbs. 6:27-28.

What does it mean to scoop fire into your lap?

When have you done this?

Day by Day

Day 3

What did you learn from this event?

Are there any areas of your life where you are lighting fires outside of the fireplace? Explain.

Are there any areas of your life where you are playing with matches? This would include any areas in your life where you are contemplating or experimenting with behaviors that you know could lead you into sin. Explain.

God's Way

Read John 14:6 and 1 Corinthians 2:14.

List as many facts as you can about Michael Jordan (or your favorite superstar) below.

Do you know this person personally or on a first name basis?

List as many facts as you can about Jesus below.

Do you know Jesus personally and intimately?

For many of us we know **about** our favorite superstar but we don't **know him.**

Unfortunately the same is often true of our relationship to Jesus. We know **about** Jesus but we don't **know him**. Below are listed some scriptures that will help you know Him on a personal basis. Read and summarize them.

John 3:16

John 10:10

Romans 3:23

Isaiah 59:2

Romans 6:23

Romans 5:8

John 14:6

Romans 10:9-10;

Romans 3:23

Day by Day

Day 4

God's Way

Read 1 Thessalonians 4:3-8 and Hebrews 13:4.

What two things do we know about regarding purity and holiness from 1 Thessalonians 4: 3 and 7?

Day by Day

Day 5

Purity is a blessing, **a blessing that gives us vision.** *"Blessed are the pure in heart for they will see God,"* (Matthew 5:8).

Have you lost your sense of God's presence in your life? Maybe it's time to check your purity. Write down anything God brings to you mind that might be keeping you from seeing Him clearly.

Purity also is **a blessing that keeps us sane.**

"At the end of that time, I, Nebuchadnezzar, raised my eyes towards heaven, and my sanity was restored. Then I praised the Most High; I honored and glorified him who lives for ever. His dominion is an eternal dominion; his kingdom endures from generation to generation" (Daniel 4:34).

"The mind of sinful man is death, but the mind controlled by the Spirit is life and peace;" (Romans 8:6).

"Furthermore, since they did not think it worthwhile to retain the knowledge of God, he gave them over to a depraved mind, to do what ought not to be done" (Romans 1:28).

Read the verse written above and write down what you learn about the relationship between sanity and purity.

Purity is **a blessing that helps us love.** *"The goal of this command is love, which comes from a pure heart and a good conscience and a sincere faith"* (I Timothy 1:5).

According to this verse, where does godly love come from?

Purity will be **a blessing to your marriage.** *"Marriage should be honored by all, and the marriage bed kept pure, for God will judge the adulterer and all the sexually immoral"* (Hebrews 13:4).

In your own words, write what this verse tells you about God's desire for your sexual relationship in marriage?

Purity is

a blessing

that helps

us love!

God's Way

Review and reflect.

Review the verse for the week and all five previous days of devotions.

What are the three biggest lessons you learned from this week's materials?

For each of those lessons, write a one-sentence statement explaining why it impressed you.

How does this material relate to staying pure and holy?

Day by Day

Day 6

CHAPTER 5   KNOW GOD'S POWER

"His divine power has given us everything we need for life and godliness through our knowledge of him who called us by his own glory and goodness. Through these he has given us his very great and precious promises, so that through them you may participate in the divine nature and escape the corruption in the world caused by evil desires" (II Peter 1:3-4).

Imagine the car of your dreams. It is sleek, loaded with extras, powerful, and it has been given to you! Not only that, but you are about to go on an awesome adventure in this car. It will be a trip full of dangerous terrain and spectacular sights and you can hardly wait to start. You get into the car, appreciating the way the seats feel, how the dashboard looks, how the stereo sounds.

You grab the wheel and begin steering. But the car's not going anywhere. You look down. You are fairly new at this driving thing, after all, and realize you need to press down on the accelerator. "That's the ticket", you say, "time for the express lane." But no. Nothing happens! What could be wrong? You realize that you forgot to change gears. "That's right I'm in Park. Let's see "N" is for..."

Oh no, now you start rolling backwards! Brake, where's the brake? You see it and slam it down, giving yourself a nice little whiplash in the process. Frustrated, thinking out loud you say, "I wish someone would have shown me how to use this thing before they gave it to me."

Sometimes, relationships can feel like that. They start out as such a gift and end up in frustration. Why is that?

"Finally, brothers, we instructed you how to live in order to please God..." (1 Thessalonians. 4:1). Going back to our theme passage, we find that God does want to give you an awesome gift, but He won't leave you to figure out for yourself how to use it or how to make it work. Unfortunately, many of us simply accept the gift and don't wait around for any instructions. Or we have the instructions, but we just don't use them. Then we wonder why we end up frustrated, and usually try to blame God for the trouble we get ourselves into.

God doesn't just shower you and me with these good and perfect gifts (James 1:17). He goes a step further and gives us instructions on how best to enjoy the gifts He gives us. We have talked about some of these things in our study together already, but there's more.

Imagine that the car we mentioned earlier is your purity. How do you get this gift to move forward? Too often those who are neutral about their purity end up rolling backwards! Maybe you could try to push it. No, all that self exertion doesn't seem to work. And it's not much fun, either. This gift was supposed to be something you enjoy! Your dreams are so big and so right. You want to go places for God and with God. How can you get moving in the direction of those dreams?

After you have completed driving school, which you decide was a great investment, you look under the hood and realize that the engine is the most important factor in what you want to do with the car. You need the power from the engine in order to move forward! Now that you realize this, you get back in the car, look at your manual, and say, "Duh, maybe I need to turn the key!" Vrrroom, "Wow, what a sweet sound!" Having taken the time to learn how to drive and how to make the car work for you, you now pull out of the driveway and onto the road of life. This is easier than you thought and much more fun than trying, in frustration, to move the car without the benefit of the power provided by the engine.

What does this illustration have to do with your purity? Everything! Many of us try to practice purity using our own strength and when we experience failure, we wonder how people ever get anywhere along the purity path. Maybe you feel like that right now. Well, there's hope. God's power is available!

God knows that we will never succeed in our practice of purity on our own and, therefore, He gives us His power. He is the engine that powers our purity and His Word tells us so. *"His divine power has given us everything we need for life and godliness..."* (II Peter 1:3). In order to put that power to work for you, you need to turn the key. In tapping into God's power source, turning the key involves only one thing: Asking!

"You do not have, because you do not ask God" (James 4:2). Prayer is our means of turning the key with God. We need to ask Him for the power needed to accomplish His will, knowing that whatever His will is, it is the best possible plan for our lives. Let's look at what God's power will enable us to do.

Power to overcome temptation.
We have talked to thousands of young people who struggle with temptation and often fall prey to it. Remember that temptation is not a sin! Giving in to it is. Imagine for a minute that your friend Maryann is home alone. As she begins to sit down to a good meal, she hears a knock at the door. Because she is a smart person, she looks through the window to see who is knocking.

"My name is Mike, and I'm a thief." How does she know that he's telling the truth? She notices that the word "Thief" is tattooed right on his forehead. "Let me in" he says, "I'm harmless...and I'm fun."

Many try to practice purity, using their own strength.

90

What should Maryann do?

You can't always choose who is going to come to your door, but you can always choose who you let in. Having a thief knock on your door isn't a sin. Opening the door and letting him steal from your family is. Letting him move in and live with you is even worse.

Temptation is just like Mike. He may come knocking, but you don't have to let him in. God's power is available to overcome temptation. Tap into that power through prayer. He will give you insight into temptation's true character and will empower you to keep the door locked and bolted so that temptation will have no choice but to move one to another victim.

Power to overcome sin.

Well, you may already have guessed that Maryann didn't take your advice. She let Mike in. It all started out to be fun and remained so just as long as Mike got his way.

"Can I have this?" Mike asked,

"Well I guess so." Maryann replied. But soon he started taking valuable things, things that mattered.

"Um, you can't have that. That's my Mom's," Maryann protested.

"Really? I'll take it anyway!"

Maryann's fear rose. "You can't take all this stuff. It doesn't belong to you."

Mike just laughed as he said, "Watch this!" and threw a chair through the living room window.

Maryann grew more alarmed and sputtered, "You're going to have to leave now."

Mike grinned maliciously, "Who's going to make me?"

What should Maryann do? What would you do? Let's look at several things that become very clear from this example:

First, overcoming temptation is always

- easier
- less costly
- and less destructive

than overcoming sin, especially if it is sin that you have invited into your life.

God's power is available to overcome temptation.

91

Second, overcoming sin always takes more:

- power
- time
- and energy

than overcoming temptation.

For Maryann to get rid of Mike, she needs more power than she has, more time than she can afford, and more energy than she wants to expend. She needs help and she needs it fast. The other element she has to contend with is the destruction factor. Even when she gets rid of Mike, she doesn't just start over where she was before she let him in. Now there is clean up and repair that has to be done. The longer she lets him stay, the worse it gets. In fact, there may be things that she can never clean, repair, or replace.

Fortunately for Maryann, her Uncle Bo lives right next door. Being a proud young woman, Maryann didn't want to call for help. She wanted to take care of this one on her own. But Mike just set the family room on fire. Realizing that she has been stupid for waiting, she turns her back on Mike, pulls out her cell phone, and dials her uncle. Mike sees what she is doing and yells, "N-O-O-O-O!" as Maryann simply cries into the receiver, "Help me..."

Uncle Bo crashes through the door almost before Maryann even gets the words out, and Mike, cringing before Bo's massiveness, says, "Well, she invited me in."

"She what?" Uncle Bo asks.

Mike replies a little more confidently, "Yeah, man, she invited me in."

Uncle Bo turns to Maryann and asks the critical question "Do you want me to take him away?"

"Why should it matter what I want?" asks Maryann.

"Because this is your house. I am not going to throw your guests out. Do you want me to take him away?"

What should she say? What would you say? *I call on the LORD in my distress, and he answers me* (Psalm 120:1). Are you calling on the Lord, or are you trying to overcome sin by your own strength? Remember the key is prayer. You need to call on God to give you His power. He always answers those who call on Him out of a pure heart. Remember what sin does—it comes between you and God. He wants to remove that barrier. You can call on Him right now, but there's a catch.

I call on the Lord

in my distress, and

he answers me.

Psalm 120:1

"But you know that he appeared so that he might take away our sins" (I John 3:5). You have to want Him to take you sin away. He will not take away what you are not ready to give up. Do you want Jesus to take your sin away? Just like Uncle Bo appeared to take away Mike, Jesus came into our lives to do the same. But, this is not just a one time or future event. He wants to take away your sin today! Do you want Him to do that? God's power is available to overcome sin. You just have to ask.

Power to know right.

"His divine power has given us everything we need for life and godliness through our knowledge of him who called us by his own glory and goodness" II Peter 1:3). Knowing right from wrong is a matter of hearing what your conscience has to say and then listening to it.

"Even when Gentiles, who do not have God's written law, instinctively follow what the law says, they show that in their hearts they know right from wrong. They demonstrate that God's law is written within them, for their own consciences either accuse them or tell them they are doing what is right" (Romans 2:14-15). Knowledge is power. The knowledge of God and His law is supernatural power. Power is not about knowing techniques, steps, or gimmicks. These things may be helpful, but they will do nothing for you if you are not connected to Jesus. Power is about knowing Jesus. To know Him is to experience the reality of who He is and rightness of His ways. However, God doesn't just want us to know what is right, He wants us to give us the power to be right.

Power to be right.

"...so that through them you may participate in the divine nature and escape the corruption in the world caused by evil desires" (II Peter 1:4).

"And he is entirely fair and just in this present time when he declares sinners to be right in his sight because they believe in Jesus" (Romans 3:26). You may know what is right and even do what is right at times, but God wants you to **be** right. He wants you to **be** the kind of person inside and outside that He desires. Loving Him and loving others is what God wants, not just with nice words, but in actions that demonstrate His awesome transforming power at work inside of you. He wants what you do to flow from who you are. It is His goal to transform you into the image of His Son. It is His goal to grow within you characteristics that are consistent with His nature so that it will be evident that you are a child of God. It is His goal for the old you to be crucified and for Christ to live out His life in and through you. You cannot reach any of God's goals for you by your own efforts, but God's power is available to you so that you can **be** right.

Power to do right.

God desires that we overcome sin and temptation. But His desire

> *His divine power has given us everything we need for life and godliness.*
> *II Peter 1:3*

doesn't stop here. He wants to help you know, be, and do right. It is easy to mistake the absence of sinful acts for the presence of righteousness. This is a mistake. Some people try to sit on the fence only to find out that there is no fence. In fact, Jesus teaches that you are experiencing one of two conditions. You are either on His side or you are against Him. Read the verses given below.

"He who is not with me is against me, and he who does not gather with me, scatters. When an evil spirit comes out of a man, it goes through arid places seeking rest and does not find it. Then it says, 'I will return to the house I left.' When it arrives, it finds the house swept clean and put in order. Then it goes and takes seven other spirits more wicked than itself, and they go in and live there. And the final condition of that man is worse than the first" (Luke 11:23-26).

If your life were a hotel, would you have a Vacancy or No Vacancy sign up?

Jesus tells us that we are with Him or against Him. There is no middle ground. Matthew says the evil spirit *"finds the house unoccupied"* or vacant (Matthew 12:44). If your life were a hotel, would you have a Vacancy or a No Vacancy sign up? If you have a Vacancy sign, then you need to invite Jesus in or else the choice will be made for you and your life will be occupied by those who are against Him. If you have a No Vacancy sign up, then who lives there? Is Jesus the occupant of your life? Here's how you can find out. Are you for Christ? How do you know that? What evidence can you point to that shows this is the case? Are you gathering for Christ? How do I know that?

When you receive Christ, God puts the Holy Spirit inside you. Your job is to work out what God has put in. Have you ever seen an apple tree? How did you know what kind of tree it was? By its fruit, right? It produces apples because it is an apple tree and its nature is to produce apples. In Christ, you produce fruit because you have a new nature and that new nature produces spiritual fruit just as surely as an apple tree produces apples. As Jesus said, *"I am the vine; you are the branches. If a man remains in me and I in him, he will bear much fruit; apart from me you can do nothing"* (John 15:5).

Jesus wants us to know Him and His righteousness and, in knowing Him in this intimate way, to be made right on the inside through Him. *"I pray that out of his glorious riches he may strengthen you with power through his Spirit in your inner being,"* (Ephesians 3:16). He wants to fill us with his Holy Spirit who gives us life and power that flows from the inside to the outside. God's power is available. Bow you head, pray to Him, tell Him you want His power to fill you and control your life. Then turn the key and hang on for a great ride!

Dig Deeper: Know God's Power

"...His divine power has given us everything we need for life and godliness..." (II Peter 1:3).

Read these verses from the Bible that support our need to rely on God's power. There is room under each verse if you want to write some power notes from the verses you read.

II Peter 1:3-4

Luke 10:19

Philippians 4:13

Micah 3:8

James 1:13-14

I Chronicles 29:12

1 Corinthians 10:13

Titus 2:12

John 10:10

Psalm 68:34

Psalm 23:4

Psalm 46:1

Proverbs 7:2

Luke 1:35

I Peter 3:21-22

John 16:33

Luke 9:1

Psalm 147:5

God _____ you.

He knows what's _____ for you.

He has the _____ to bring it about.

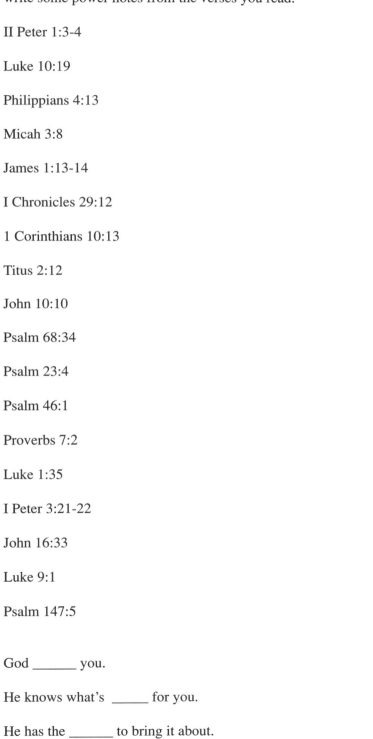

We spend too much of life trying to do things in our own power.

Journal Page

Take Action

Pray asking God to identify a statement and/or scripture that was meaningful to you in this chapter.

On your journal page, write this statement or scripture passage as well as any other thoughts or feelings you have in response to what you are learning.

Know God's Power

Memory Verse: *"His divine power has given us everything we need for life and godliness through our knowledge of him who called us by his own glory and goodness. Through these he has given us his very great and precious promises, so that through them you may participate in the divine nature and escape the corruption in the world caused by evil desires"* (II Peter 1:3-4).

Read II Peter 1:3-4.

Describe "his divine power" as well as you can in your own words. Don't worry if you are not sure how to describe it; great theologians struggle over understanding this concept.

List some of the great and precious promises of God's Word.

How will the first half of this scripture help you escape corruption caused by evil desires?

Day by Day

Day 1

Why do so many people fail in their efforts to escape this corruption? (see verse 4)

Know God's Power

Read II Corinthians 4: 7-10.

What is the "treasure" referred to in verse 7? (see verses 5-6)

How do people see that our power comes from God? How much do we try to do on our own?

Day by Day

Day 2

According to verses 8 and 9, what are some of the challenges that face us?

How does God's power help us in facing those challenges?

List any ways that you think someone else has seen God's power at work in you.

Know God's Power

Read Isaiah 40: 28-31.

According to verse 28, what are two things the Lord will not do?

What does He give to those who need it?

Describe the picture that is painted of those who call on God's power.

How does this passage relate to purity and holiness in relationships?

Day by Day

Day 3

Know God's Power

Read Ephesians 3:20-21, Ephesians 1:19-20, and Colossians 1: 28-29.

What does Ephesians 3:20 say about how much Christ can accomplish in our lives?

Day by Day

Day 4

How does He accomplish these things?

List ways that He has done immeasurably more in your life than you could ask or think.

Describe the power that is available to us as told in Ephesians 1:19-20.

Paul was known as a great evangelist. In Colossians 1:28-29, to what does he credit his success in ministry?

What are some ways you can surrender and yield to God's power?

Know God's Power

Read Psalm 46:1-3, Psalm 68:34, and Psalm 147:5.

According to Psalm 46:1, when is God's power available to us?

List the catastrophes of Psalm 46:2-3.

List some of the catastrophes you or your friends have experienced.

How might these verses apply to a catastrophic relationship in which someone may have been involved?

From Psalm 68:34-35 and Psalm 147:5, list some ways you have seen God's power at work. How can you better realize and utilize God's power?

Day by Day

Day 5

Know God's Power

Review and reflect.

Review the verse for the week and all five previous days of devotions.

What are the three biggest lessons you learned from this week's materials?

Day by Day

Day 6

For each of those lessons, write a one-sentence statement explaining why it impressed you.

How does this material relate to staying pure and holy?

CHAPTER 6   FIND FRIENDS WHO ARE IN AGREEMENT

I Corinthians 15:33 says, *"Do not be deceived, evil company corrupts good habits"* (NKJV). The power of friendship to influence us for either good or evil is real. Detention centers, unemployment lines, jails and prisons are crowded with people who have been helped there by 'friends' who were out for themselves. The need to find friends who are in agreement with your standards and with your commitment to God, friends who will cheer for you and stand with you in the tough times, is crucial in the move to purity and holiness.

Ten qualities of a good friend

1. True friends say hard things in love.

Proverbs 25:11 says, *"A word aptly spoken is like apples of gold in settings of silver."* The verse certainly paints a beautiful picture of right words. A friend who is willing to say the right thing to you, whether it is in encouragement or in disapproval, moves the friendship beyond selfishness to a caring consideration of what is best for you. You not only need friends like that, but you need to be a friend to others in the same spirit of responsibility. You need to be able to hear and to give the aptly spoken words of a friend.

You don't revel at the thought of those embarrassing moments when you found out your pants were split, you had a stain on your clothes, your face had dirt on it, or any one of a number of similar predicaments in which you may have found yourself. Yet, you were thankful when a friend quietly came alongside and made you aware of your predicament. If our friends did not inform us and we found out in some other way, we would have scolded them for not helping. If their reply was, "I was afraid you might be offended," we would have said something to the effect that it was better to be offended than to be humiliated.

The same is true in the more significant issues of life. A word of love from a friend may confront your attitude of bitterness, anger, or hatred toward another. Honesty, integrity and a sense of honorableness may be seen as hard and narrow-minded, but they are characteristics that are needed as we move forward in true friend relationships. A word of correction regarding honoring your parents is expected from other adults and maybe accepted with reservations. But when a peer challenges your attitudes and motives, you are more likely to listen to and respond to the challenge.

2. True friends lead and follow to the right places.

Joshua 24:15 says, *"But, as for me and my household, we will serve the Lord."* True friends learn that there is a time to step up and lead, and another time not only to follow, but also to encourage the leadership of another.

Natural leaders run to the forefront and often struggle to step back and allow someone else to lead. The quiet follower is content to sit back and allow others to lead on. Great friendships encourage the growth of each other. A friend not jealous and actually rejoices in the good fortunes of another friend. For some it may mean encouraging the quieter person to step up, while the more aggressive personality willingly steps back from a leadership role. When a healthy balance is achieved, both friends are blessed and God's work gets accomplished.

Two friends were at odds. When confronted with the conflict, the first said, "He is always trying to boss me around. We never do anything I want to do. I'm sick of it."

The second retorted, "Are you crazy? Every time I ask what you want to do, you say, 'I don't care.' I'm tired of having to be the one who makes the decisions." After a short period of sorting out the issues, they came to realize that they had settled into a pattern. As they discussed their goals for themselves and their friendship, they realized that each needed to encourage the other to properly lead at some times and to be a willing follower at others.

3. True friends demand the best from one another.

Proverbs 27: 17 says, *"As iron sharpens iron, so one man sharpens another."* A true friend is not threatened when another friend excels in a particular area, but instead encourages and celebrates the maximum effort and success of the one who is doing so well. True friends rejoice together and do not see themselves as competing against each other.

Everyone needs celebrators in his life. A true friend sees all that his friend can do and encourages him to go for it while he stands ready to assist and give feedback. In today's world, comparisons and egos stop people from helping others to develop to their full potential. When iron sharpens iron, there is some friction involved. So it is in a true and honest friendship. There may be moments of friction, but the end result is a sharper, more useable instrument.

I recall sitting in the car with a good friend as I described some challenges I was facing in my life. He looked at me and said, "I see the following red flags waving ...." He went on to lay out his concerns. At the end he asked, "What are you going to do about it, and how can I help?" I was sharpened by my friend that day.

Do not be deceived, evil company corrupts good habits.

I Corinthians 15:33
(NKJV)

4. True friends promote doing the right things.

II Timothy 2:22 says, *"Flee the evil desires of youth, and pursue righteousness, faith, love and peace, along with those who call on the Lord out of a pure heart."* True friends help each other to discern the proper time to do the proper things.

The Bible commands, *"He who has ears, let him hear."* (Matthew 13:9). Someone once said that if God gave us two ears and only one mouth, then should we listen twice as much as we speak. I have to agree with that conclusion. Over the years we have spoken to thousands of young people. Often we can look out in the crowd and see a couple of friends who are intent on distracting each other as well as those around them. In those instances, those trying to listen find it difficult to quiet those who are focused on distraction.

In one particular group, there was a young man who was a constant distraction. I tried moving him to other locations. I had quiet talks with him about this problem and even made the suggestion he not attend the sessions. It also became noticeable that he was attempting to catch the eye of a certain young lady. She came to me with her frustration about his constant distractions. After some initial conversation with her, I suggested that the next time he acted up, she quietly but firmly ask him to be quiet and quit disturbing her. She agreed to do so.
When we were at the next service, the same scenario unfolded, until she poked him and said, "Would you please be quiet, I am trying to listen." If I had videotaped the event, the next few frames would reveal a young man who melted right then and there. His conduct throughout the remainder of the weekend was wonderful. Later, he thanked her for the reprimand. Indeed he had listened and made wise decisions as a result. But the correction was more clearly heard and accepted from a friend than it was from an adult. Friends have great influence over friends.

Friends have great influence over friends.

5. True friends draw even closer in tough times.

Proverbs 17:17 says, *"A friend loves at all times, and a brother is born for adversity."* The norm, in today's world, is that when times get tough, people who may have called themselves friends scatter and become scarce. On the other hand, many people have shared that their greatest moments of friendship were not shared through words or activities, but rather through the simple presence of a dear friend during a tough time. True friends have learned from experience that it is not what they say but where they are that counts the most during a friend's greatest hours of need.

What do we do when there are no words to express our thoughts? In the face of true suffering and pain, words can be very empty. At those times, we are often needed by our friends the most. So many young people I have spoken with express sorrow about not having the right words to say in difficult times. When asked what they do in such situations, they usually respond, "I don't do anything. I just avoid them." The opposite should be the case. True friends, during the times of struggle, simply make themselves available. If friendship is evaluated by wonderful words during tough times, then we are all doomed. It's not the words you say, it is the friendship support that you are willing to give. Be there.

When I was in college, a former girlfriend's brother died of cancer. About five of my buddies from school rode with me to the funeral home. The line to see the family at the casket was long. As we waited, we talked. As we progressed toward the front where the family stood, one by one my friends excused themselves from line. When we were within about three people of reaching the parents of the young man who had died, my best friend looked at me and said, "They don't really know me. I'll meet you at the back." I felt alone and clueless as to what to say. To this day I remember no words I uttered to either the parents or the girl. About two weeks later, the girl called to tell me that her parents had asked that she call to thank me for coming. They had noticed my friends leaving the line and simply wanted me to know that my coming had been a blessing. Once again, it is often not what we say, but where we are that counts.

6. True friends ask for and grant forgiveness.

James 5:16 says, *"Therefore confess your sins to each other and pray for each other so that you may be healed. The prayer of a righteous man is powerful and effective."* Forgiveness is a two-way street. First, the true friend is willing to ask for forgiveness. Second, the true friend is quick to grant forgiveness when he has been wronged.

Some people are better at asking for forgiveness than they are in granting it. When we have been wronged, there is a tendency to desire to hang on to the feelings of anger or bitterness even after forgiveness has been sought. We seem to want to store up the offense for future reference. In the same way, for many of us, the words, "Will you forgive me?" get stuck somewhere in the throat area. We may feel the need in our heart for forgiveness, but to get the request out as words is another adventure. True friends need to learn to take the brave step of putting words of forgiveness into their vocabulary.

When forgiveness is sought from us, and we grant it, we must move on. To store up negative feelings about the incident only hurts us. Stored up unforgiveness festers within us and spreads like an infection. Then when it comes out of us, it is usually nasty and hurtful to others. There is no way to have a close friendship with anyone and not, at some time, need to ask for or to give

It is often not what we say, but where we are that counts.

forgiveness. Our ability to do this openly and honestly is crucial to our personal wellbeing and to the health of our friendship.

7. True friends are consistent.

They are the same in public as they are in private. Hebrews 13: 7, 8 says, *"Remember your leaders, who spoke the word of God to you. Consider the outcome of their way of life and imitate their faith. Jesus Christ is the same yesterday and today and forever."*

A young lady once approached me in tears. She had just passed her best friend in the hallway at school. As she passed by, she heard her friend criticizing and mocking her. When the two next met, the friend who had been so critical shrugged it off and said "Everybody talks about everybody when they're not around." Unfortunately, in today's world, that appears to be all too true. But, we would suggest to you that true friends behave consistently whether in private or in public. The encouraging news is that Jesus, who is the greatest example of the true friend, is the same yesterday, today, and forever. Consistency is something we all desire. We look for someone we can count on, someone we can trust, and someone who always accepts us for who we are.

One of the greatest challenges to consistency comes in how we handle gossip. People love juicy stories, and can't wait to share them with the next available set of ears. More damage is done to friendships by talking behind backs than by anything that happens face-to-face. Be careful about your words. Be the same person in front of your friends as you are behind them. We need to strive toward becoming friends who are consistent. Look for that kind of friends. Pray that you will find one and then take the steps needed to be one.

> *"... Jesus Christ is the same yesterday and today and forever."*
>
> *Hebrews 13:8*

8. True friends are recyclable.

They are willing to be used over and over again. Proverbs 18:24 says, *"A man of many companions may come to ruin, but there is a friend who sticks closer than a brother."*

Notice, we did not say they are willing to be abused over and over again. There is a difference between being used and being abused. A true friend desires to be a helper. When an opportunity arises to help, there's a sense of joy that comes in being able to serve the other friend. When the situation requiring help is over, the helping friend does not say, "You owe me!" Instead, the friend says, "Don't hesitate to call if I can help again."

Several years ago one of the staffers of the camp that I work for was traveling during a snowstorm in Michigan. His car slid off the road near the home of a friend of the camp. Not quite sure what to do, the staffer called the camp and asked for suggestions. A call was made to the nearby friend who brought out his four-wheel-drive truck, pulled the car out of the ditch, and escorted the staffer to another friend's house. That friend then fed him and provided a bed for the night. In the morning, the friend escorted him down the road with the words, "If you ever need help like that again, don't hesitate to call." And he meant it! Those people showed themselves to be recyclable friends. True friends are excited about the opportunity to help. True friends see such events not as inconveniences but as opportunities.

9. True friends are thankful people.

Colossians 3:17 says, *"And whatever you do, whether in word or deed, do it all in the name of the Lord Jesus, giving thanks to God the Father through him."*

It is hard to have a heart of thankfulness and then have our actions show bitterness or anger. Instead, we find that thankfulness breeds thankfulness. Thankful people tend to smile and laugh and enjoy life. Their moments together are marked with positive conversations, concern for others, and the enjoyment of being together.

I would challenge you to develop a list of things for which you can be thankful. An old-time hymn says, "A thousand, a thousand thanksgivings I bring, blessed Savior to thee." One year, during the Thanksgiving season, a gentleman challenged me to write down 1,000 items for which I could offer thanksgiving. Making that list changed my perspective on giving thanks. I found myself driving down the road looking for things for which I was thankful. I wrote a letter to an older gentleman who had been a wonderful example to me. In the letter I said, "Just wanted you to know that you are #38 on my thankful list. You're right between Coney dogs and bathroom tissue."

When I saw him in church the next Sunday he said, "I see I'm keeping pretty select company."

What is the norm for your conversations with friends? If they are marked with criticism and complaints, throw up a caution flag. Then determine how you can move to a more thankful pattern. Remember, true friends need to be thankful people. With that understanding, we will lead each other to thankfulness.

10. True friends accept other friends.

Friends and friends of friends are inclusive, not exclusive. John 1:41-42 says, *"The first thing Andrew did was to find his brother Simon (Peter) and tell him, 'We have found the Messiah' ... Then he brought him to Jesus ...* (parentheses added). Notice that the less flamboyant Andrew brought his very flamboyant brother, Peter, to the Lord. Andrew's life was marked as being the bringer. He continually brought people to Jesus.

Too many times a boyfriend/girlfriend relationship becomes exclusive. The couple wants to spend all their time together to the point of deliberate exclusion of others. Her friends and/or his friends are no longer part of the mix. If she talks with her friends or spends time with them, she may be chastised and told, "You are my girl."

It shouldn't be that way. Instead, we would suggest that true friends improve other friendships. If we use the example of Christ as our best friend, it is obvious that my relationships to others should improve and deepen because of my relationship with Him.

Relationships involve risks. Too many friendships are selfishly possessive. When we find a really good friend, we can become fearful of losing him. As soon as we take on that fear, we are tempted to become more exclusive in our time together.

Have you ever held a handful of nice, white beach sand? If you value that sand, you might think about taking it and squeezing it hard so you can make sure you don't lose it. The problem is that the harder you squeeze the handful of sand, the more of it you lose. You probably have witnessed many 'squeezed friendships' fall apart. But if a friendship feels really good, thoughts run through our minds that say, "I don't want to share." "I'm afraid I'll lose this friend." Or "If I can keep everyone else away, this will be a friend for life." The reality is that expanding our friendships is the best way to develop long-lasting and meaningful relationships.

...choose friends who cheer for you, celebrate with you and desire to see you prosper in your walk with God.

While we all look for committed friends, the greater question should be asked, "Am I the kind of friend I am looking for?" If we were to hold Jesus up to these ten qualities, you would find a perfect match. Our challenge to you is to think about the steps you need to take to be the kind of friend we have described in this chapter, the kind of friend that Jesus is to us. We guarantee that anyone who sincerely strives after these qualities will become a sought after friend. Instead of looking outward, we need to take time to look inward. The first step to finding friends who are in agreement is to become a friend of character.

Over the years qualities of good friends other than those we have described here have been suggested, such as: True friends are not perfect, true friends are real, and true friends are transparent. The list could go on, but the essence of true friendship remains critical. Know that the a life of purity and holiness is made easier by finding friends who are in agreement with that commitment and those goals. Desire friends and choose friends who cheer for you, celebrate with you, and desire to see you prosper in your walk with God.

Special note.

Many young people have asked us what to do about friends who are not in agreement. This chapter may lead you to hard decisions about making changes in friendships in which you are involved. Conversations you have with these friends who are not in agreement with your commitment can be hurtful, tough, and something that you desire to avoid. Yet for some of you, leaving behind friendships that are destructive to you is a decision that must be made if you are committed to following God's leading.

The first steps are the toughest ones. The fear of never finding any other friends is real, but the consequences of staying in bad friendships are much more severe than the problem of finding new friends. Over the years we've heard success stories that encourage and verify that choosing the right friends and leaving behind the friends who are not in agreement is the right move. The reality that God does fulfill His promises needs to be understood. When Philippians 4:19 says, *"And my God will meet all of your needs according to his glorious riches in Christ Jesus"*, He will do exactly that. To believe in anything less is to minimize who God is and not to take seriously what He has promised to do for you.

And my God will meet all of your needs according to his riches in glory.

Philippians 4:19

Evangelistic dating.
Many times we have heard people state that they would like to date someone who is close to becoming a Christian. We call it 'evangelistic dating'. We have witnessed many of these relationships through the years and can tell you that, in almost all cases, they become destructive. If you are ever considering evangelistic dating, you should take the following steps.

First, you should read II Corinthians 6:14-18 to understand God's instruction about close relationships between believers and unbelievers.

Second, you should find someone else (maybe a youth leader or a godly adult) of the same sex as the person whom you wish to date and encourage that stronger or older Christian to share the gospel with the non-Christian. It is sheer ego to think that you are the only one who could reach this person for Christ.

Next, you should work to develop a godly friendship with the person you wish to date but the boyfriend/girlfriend mentality needs to be avoided.

Finally, if the other person insists on a boyfriend/girlfriend or nothing relationship, the only reasonable choice is nothing.

Several years ago, a young woman, told me that her boyfriend was close to becoming a Christian. His words to her were, "I can't do it without you. I need you here to help me." After much discussion and prayer, I told her that unless she broke off the relationship, she would probably be pregnant within a year. Less than one year later, she called to inform me of their upcoming wedding and, indeed, her pregnancy. The relationship faltered and eventually failed with a son and daughter left to be raised by a single mother. We must avoid doing wrong things even for what seem like good reasons. The measuring stick for making all such decisions must be the Bible.

In conclusion.
We started this chapter with the reminder from I Corinthians 15:33, that evil company corrupts good habits. The company we keep is a key factor to purity and holiness. The illustration is often used of a strong young man standing on a chair and a weaker one lying on the ground. They grasp arms in an attempt to pull each other in their respective directions. You can guess what happens! It is easier to pull someone down than it is to bring someone up. Make wise decisions regarding friendships.

Make wise decisions regarding friendships.

Dig Deeper: Finding Friends Who Are in Agreement

It is God's will that you should be sanctified; that you should avoid sexual immorality; that each of you should learn to control his own body in a way that is holy and honorable (1 Thessalonians 4:3-4).

Circle one word from each group below that best describes you.

Group One

Encouraging
Initiating
Clarifying

Group Two

Compromising
Coordinating
 Systematizing

Group Three

Helping
Commanding
Evaluating

Group Four

Pressing for results
Gathering data
Expressing warmth

Why did you choose these particular words to describe yourself?

Write a brief evaluation of yourself in each of the areas listed below.

Physical -

Mental/Intellectual -

Emotional -

Spiritual -

A habit is a practical outworking of my personality, my strengths, and my weaknesses. In the columns below, describe BEHAVIORS that you may be engaged in that could be harmful or helpful in your efforts toward purity and holiness.

GOOD   BAD

Ask yourself if each of these habits or behaviors is helping you to be pure and holy or if any of them are hurting your purity and holiness goals. Write your response below.

A habit is a practical outworking of your personality.

Journal Page

Finding Friends Who Are in Agreement

Memory Verse
Examine yourselves to see whether you are in the faith; test yourselves. Do you not realize that Christ Jesus is in you---unless of course you fail the test (II Corinthians 13:5).

Read Romans 12:6-8, I Corinthians 12:4-6, and Ephesians 4:11-13.

List some of the spiritual gifts described in these three references.

Do you consider yourself to have gifts? Why or why not?

From your list, record what you believe to be your strongest gifts.

How can these gifts be put to good use?

Day by Day

Day 1

How can knowing your gifts help you in purity and holiness?

Finding Friends Who Are in Agreement

Read Lamentations 3:40, Matthew 7:5, I Corinthians 11:27-32, and II Corinthians 13:5.

Write in your own words verse 40 of Lamentations 3.

What is difficult about examining oneself?

From Matthew 7, why do you think it is easy to see the speck in a brother's eye and more difficult to see the log (plank) in your own?

From II Corinthians 13:5, how do you know if you have "failed the test"?

Why are we told to examine ourselves prior to taking communion?

Day by Day

Day 2

Finding Friends Who Are in Agreement

Read Proverbs 28:26, Hosea 10:13, Matthew 26:33, Luke 18:9-14, and I Corinthians 10:12.

After reading the above references, list some of the consequences of being self-confident.

How are "walking in wisdom" and "trusting in yourself" different?

Describe the parable of Luke 18:9-14.

Describe the events that took place between Jesus and Peter in Matthew 26:31-35 and 69-75.

What is the difference between self-confidence and confidence in Christ?

Day by Day

Day 3

Finding Friends Who Are in Agreement

Read Matthew 16:24-26, John 15:12-13, and Colossians 3:5-10.

Define self-denial and sacrifice.

Describe the attitude of someone who tries to act like he/she is practicing self-denial and sacrifice, but isn't.

Day by Day

Day 4

Answer the two powerful questions of Matthew 16:26.

After you read John 15:12-13, list ways you need to improve in loving others.

From Colossians 3:5, list the things we are told to put to death. From verse 8, list those things we are to rid ourselves of.

What are some areas you must work on related to denial and sacrifice?

Finding Friends Who Are in Agreement

Read Titus 2:11-14 and I John 3:16-18.

What does Titus 2:11 tell you about how to learn to say "no" to ungodliness and worldly passions?

What does verse 14 mean when it talks about being, "eager to do what is good"?

What stops you from developing an eagerness to do what is good?

How does the message of I John 3:18 impact purity and holiness?

List two ways in which you will work to improve your path to purity and holiness. Be specific, keeping in mind your weaknesses.

Day by Day

Day 5

How can you use your strengths to your advantage in the purity and holiness journey?

Finding Friends Who Are in Agreement

Review and reflect.

Review the verse for the week and all five previous days of devotions.

What are the three biggest lessons you learned from this week's materials?

For each of those lessons, write a one-sentence statement explaining why it impressed you.

How does this material relate to staying pure and holy?

Day by Day

Day 6

Seeking help is not a sign of weakness, but rather a sign of maturity. The world is full of destroyed lives of people who thought they could handle things on their own. There are many examples in the Bible of more mature believers helping those who were younger either in age or in the faith. For example, the Bible tells us about Paul training Timothy. In fact, when Paul was in prison and about to be killed, the very last letters he wrote were to Timothy, the young man Paul had carefully trained to take over the ministry that he was leaving behind. In the Old Testament, a sixteen-year-old king named Uzziah was mentored by a man named Zechariah, who, scripture tells us, instructed him in the fear of the Lord. Other passages show Elijah bringing Elisha alongside his ministry in order to train him. Samuel heard God speak and went to Eli for counsel. The list of biblical examples goes on and on. Today's world has labeled this kind of teaching as mentoring, discipling or having an accountability partner, among other terms. Just know that the concept of finding someone to hold you accountable or someone to lead you by teaching and example is not new to this generation.

Imagine that you are sitting in a school classroom and your teacher enters just as class is about to begin. From the back of his pants comes a line of toilet paper. The class soon begins to rumble and to laugh at this poor man's predicament. As he arrives at the front of the room, he sneezes into his hands leaving a shiny mucus film on the tips of his moustache. So there he is, the toilet paper is still protruding and a mess on his moustache. The crowd laughter increases as one student quietly takes him aside and says, "Excuse me, let me help you."

He responds, "Is something wrong?"

"Well, when you sneezed – well, here take this tissue and wipe your face. That's right, just a little more right there."

With a look of fear on his face he asks, "Do you think anyone noticed? Is it all off now?"

The student encouragingly adds, "you look fine, but may I share something else with you?"

"Oh no, there's not something else wrong is there?", he asks.

Very quietly the student whispers, "You have some toilet paper coming out the back of your pants."

With that announcement the teacher whirls around, grabs the

paper, and tries to hide. "Oh, I know everyone saw me, and I feel like such a fool. Do you think they are all laughing at me?"

The student assures him that we all have embarrassing things happen, and everything will be okay.

"Thank you," he says to the student. "What would I have done without your help?"

As you think about that incident, ask yourself if you can look back on a time when you wish someone had opened your eyes to some shortcoming of which you were unaware? I am sure you can think of something! We all have been in situations where we needed someone who cared about us to tell us the truth even if the truth was difficult to hear. There is no doubt that we need people in our lives who will be honest with us and will hold us accountable for living a life true to the values we endorse.

There are shortcomings and weaknesses in our lives to which we are blind, but they are things that others can see and may be able to help us overcome. How many embarrassing, problematic, and sometimes even devastating situations could be avoided if we were willing to submit to godly mentorship?

Two crucial factors exist as we study the need for accountability. First, we must be willing to find someone we trust and ask that person to guide us through some of the pitfalls we can find ourselves falling into. The best way is to determine during the good times who that person would be and get connected with him or her. If we wait until we are facing a crisis, we will not have the energy and good sense to look for such person.

During my days as a high-school counselor, I would station myself in the hallway between classes as 1,200 students moved past me. If I saw a student whom I knew because I had done some counseling work with him, it wasn't hard to sense when he was in crisis. The closer he came to my location, the more determined he appeared to look away from me. After a few days of having him avoid eye contact with me, I would call him over to my side, and ask if I had done anything to offend them. I would jokingly volunteer to change deodorant brands, use a different mouthwash, or overhaul my wardrobe. The student would grin and assure me that I had done nothing offensive. After a few minutes of conversation, the inevitable question came from my mouth. "Something has gone wrong. What's the matter? "A trip to my office followed where a tale of sorrow was usually shared. Good mentors will be able to pick up when they are being ignored and will be able to reach out to the one being mentored in order to restore the relationship and keep the mentoree on the right track.

Needing a mentor.
Why do you need a mentor? The concept of a mentor parallels

Determine during the good times who an accountability person could be.

that of a guide. A guide is someone who is ahead of you on the journey, knows the direction in which to travel, and has found ways to successfully avoid the potholes in the road ahead. A mentor will teach you about how to make wise life decisions, will encourage your spiritual growth, and will hold you accountable for living a life in obedience to God's Word.

A mentor will not preach at you, but will show you by example and with loving guidance how to live your life successfully. He or she may also be known as an accountability partner because he has to be able to confront you if you are straying from your spiritual or personal commitments. A good mentor will carefully guide you back onto the path to which you commit when you are making wise decisions.

Finding a mentor.
As mentioned earlier, it is crucial to find a suitable mentor during the good times. The right time to act is when your thoughts are positive, the desire to do things right is high, and you clearly see the need to have such a person in your life. If you wait until a crisis arrives (and it will!), emotions will always win over what you know you should do. Make the decision to place yourself in an accountability relationship when the head and heart are in proper alignment.

How do you find the right mentor? First, sit down and develop a list of names of people who could and would hold you accountable. Characteristics of such a person should be as follows:

1. Same sex.

    We recommend that the person you choose as a mentor be the same sex as you are. Why? The struggles you face are usually best discussed with someone who has experienced similar situations in life. Women tend to understand and relate better to the challenges of a female teen. In the same way, men will resonate with a young man's questions. Same sex mentorship also opens the door for frank discussion about matters that would be more difficult to share with the opposite sex.

2. Older than you.

    Also, the person you ask should be older than you are. Why? In many situations, things that need to be shared are best shared with someone who is removed from the immediate situation. One young man asked his best friend to be his accountability partner. The first time he shared a struggle with his friend about a certain young lady, the conversation became cold and withdrawn. Upon further examination, the mentor-friend confessed that he also had romantic feelings about the young lady being discussed. All of a sudden, his desire to help his friend became secondary to his own

A guide is someone who is ahead of you on the journey.

feelings. When an accountability person is someone older, those conflicts are removed entirely. Also, an older person has a greater depth of personal experience and is usually able to provide a more objective perspective on any given situation than someone of your own age can do.

3.   Accessible.

Is this person someone who has the ability to be available throughout the week? While the ideal person may be willing and able, his inaccessibility may limit his effectiveness. People at a distance can assist in holding us accountable. Through phone conversations, an occasional visit, and the internet, they can be effective. However, if all circumstances are relatively equal, preference should go to someone who is more accessible.

4.   Experienced.

Does this person understand your strengths and weaknesses? Can he or she relate to the kinds of things you may experience in your young adult life? Is this prospective mentor willing to confront you without being obnoxious?

5.   Willing.

It is always best to find someone who is not only willing but also enthusiastic about the opportunity. You may need to encourage the person by being specific about why you think he would be a good mentor for you. That encouragement may be all he needs to be willing to begin this walk with you.

It is always best to find someone not only willing, but also enthusiastic about the opportunity.

Can a parent be an effective mentor? The immediate answer is 'yes'. Parents should be accountability partners even without your specific request that they do so. Parents need to be active in the life of their children and, for the most part, they want to take a positive teaching and accountability role. If a young person makes such a request of a parent, it can be a moment of great exhilaration for Mom or Dad as it takes off some of the pressure of their constantly wondering if they are being too intrusive in their child's growing years. So, parents are one great source of mentoring and accountability.

Even though parents can play a crucial role in your development, having as a mentor another person outside the family realm can also be helpful. Finding another who desires to come alongside in support and love can be a great asset, not only to you, but to your family as well. It is a wise family which encourages the involvement of their young person with a trusted advisor outside the family unit.

Asking a mentor.
Do you have a list of several prospective mentors now? If not, you

may need to stop at this point and make that list. Then, schedule a meeting with your first choice from that list and request that person's assistance in your life journey. When you meet with your chosen mentor, you may need to encourage him or her to be willing to hold you accountable and be your teacher. Explain what you need to have this person do. (We will cover more about the mentor's role later in this chapter.) While an individual will undoubtedly be honored by such a request, many times he may also feel incompetent, unqualified, and overwhelmed to respond to your invitation. If you meet with that kind of resistance, encourage your chosen mentor to step out in faith and trust that God will work through him for the benefit of both of you. If the first person on your list is not able to fulfill the role, move on to your second choice and so on until you find a person who is just the one that God has put in your life.

After one particularly positive purity and holiness seminar, a teen requested accountability from a man in his seventies. This was a gentleman who was greatly respected by this teen. The gentleman refused the request because he felt he was too old. To hold someone accountable simply means a willingness to pray, be available, and ask hard questions. I am convinced that the gentleman had great wisdom and experience to share, of which the teen was highly desirous and that he missed a great opportunity to have an influence for good in the young man's life.

Don't delay.
If you are serious about finding an accountability partner, move now to begin that relationship. Don't put it off. You never know what crisis in life is just around the corner and for which you will need guidance and accountability. Good mentoring relationships take awhile to mature. Begin now so when the advice and teaching is needed most, then you will already be well positioned to receive it from someone you have grown to trust and love.

Don't

put

it

off!

Ideally, the mentor you choose is someone after whom you would like to model your life at least to some degree. Is there anyone you can think of who will help you stay pure and holy? You will find the support will help you grow in all areas of your walk with Jesus Christ if you are obedient to God in this area and follow the biblical pattern we described in the opening paragraphs of this chapter.

Over the years we've found certain people to be most effective as accountability partners. The qualities list above should lead you on the right road to selecting the right person. We recommend that you think through this process carefully, rely on God's promise that He will supply your need, and pray faithfully as you make your list. Often parents, youth leaders, and pastors can help with recommendations and assist you in this process.

Many active and vibrant and churches today are developing plans to train accountability people for their youth and for their adults. Just as Timothy needed Paul's mentorship in order to grow in wisdom and knowledge, so young people today need such training and accountability in order to grow into spiritually and emotionally healthy adults.

Accountability questions.

Your potential accountability partner might ask if you have a list of good questions they could ask when working with you. If so, tell them that our first words of advice are, "Be yourself. Do what comes naturally." A caring question such as "How are you doing?" is better than a well-worded question that comes from a textbook.

A woman shared her accountability experience in these words. "Just prior to Sally getting married, she came and thanked me for holding her and Bill accountable over the past two years. I looked at her and apologized, thinking I had done a poor job. Sally replied, 'Oh no, there was one Sunday when Bill and I were struggling in our physical relationship. That day you came up to me and asked how it was going with me and Bill.

I told you fine, but it wasn't. That day I went to Bill and said we need to work this out and do it right. I don't ever want to have to lie to that lady again. You helped set us on the right track that day. Thank you.' I learned then that the simplest question can have a great impact."

However, if your mentor would like some guidance in the kinds of questions to ask, this list of discussion starters might be helpful:

> How were you tested this week, month, or since we last met?
>
> What has God taught you from his Word or from your experience lately?
>
> What is the greatest struggle you are currently encountering?
>
> Share the story of a victory with me.
>
> Have you grown in treating others with respect and dignity? How?
>
> Have you viewed, read or listened to material that is objectionable?
>
> How does your physical appearance reflect godliness?
>
> Are you harboring any feelings of anger, bitterness or resentment?
>
> Describe your treatment of those people closest to you.
>
> What is the one thing you most fear telling me?
>
> At any time during this conversation have you lied to me?

The simplest questions can have a great impact.

When?

Is it still the desire of your heart to move towards purity and holiness?

Another tool that might be helpful for you and your mentor to use is the GROWTH Formula. Using the word *growth* as an acronym, your mentor can ask you the following questions:

G How are you GROWING in your walk with the Lord?

R How is your RELATIONSHIP with God? Others? Yourself?

O What OTHER areas of your life should I be questioning?

W How is your WORSHIP, WORK, and WORD?
    Are you seeking to WORSHIP God?
    Are you getting the job done at WORK?
    Are you in the WORD?

T How are your TIME and TALENTS being used?
    How much TIME did you spend in the Word this week?
    How did you use your TALENTS for the Lord this week?

H What is the condition of your HEART?

Are you

concerned

about

GROWTH?

Dig Deeper: Finding Support

"As iron sharpens iron, so one man sharpens another."
(Proverbs 27:17).

Read these verses:

Acts 2:42	I John 1:7	Proverbs 27:17
Ecclesiastes 4:9-10	I Samuel 18:1	Ruth 1:16
I Corinthians 15:33		

List 10 characteristics of a good friend that you find in these verses.

1)   6)
2)   7)
3)   8)
4)   9)
5)   10)

Describe below how you rate yourself as a good friend.

As iron sharpens

iron, so one man

sharpens another.

Proverbs 27:17

Journal Page

Finding Support

Memory Verse
"As iron sharpens iron, so one man sharpens another."
(Proverbs 27:17).

Day by Day

Day 1

Read Ephesians 4:15-16 and Joshua 24:15.

What does verse 15 of Ephesians 4 say a true friend will do?

How does a true friend say hard things in love?

Describe a time when a friend said something to you that was hard to hear, but you know he or she said it in love.

In Joshua 24:15 what were the circumstances that caused Joshua to make such a strong statement?

If true friends lead and follow to the right places, where was Joshua trying to lead his friends?

What are some of the difficulties in leading and following with friends?

Finding Support

Read Proverbs 27:17 and II Timothy 2:22.

What do you think Proverbs 27:17 means to people today?

What are the best ways friends can help sharpen each other?

What are the difficulties in sharpening each other?

List the qualities in II Timothy 2:22 that we should be helping each other pursue.

If true friends promote listening and doing the right things, how can those activities and actions be done with a pure heart?

List one thing you could suggest to a friend to help him/her promote any of the II Timothy 2:22 qualities.

Day by Day

Day 2

Finding Support

Read Proverbs 17:17 and James 5:16.

According to Proverbs 17:17, how often does a friend love?

What are some of the hardest times to love a friend?

Day by Day

Day 3

If the love of a true friend gets better during tough times, what are some of the toughest times you can think of? How have you done at loving your friend during those times?

In James 5:16, how is a friend instructed to act in the face of another's sin?

Which is harder, to ask for forgiveness or to grant someone forgiveness?

Why do we need to be ready to do both?

Finding Support

Read Hebrews 13:7-8 and Proverbs 18:24.

Who serves as the great example of a true friend?

Why do many friends not behave toward each other the same in private as they do in public?

True friends are recyclable (willing to be used over and over). Explain this statement in view of Proverbs 18:24

Explain this expression, "God doesn't expect friends to keep score."

How should friends celebrate victories with other friends? Why can this be difficult?

Day by Day

Day 4

Finding Support

Read Colossians 3:17 and John 15:14-15.

Based on Colossians 3:17, what should be the mark of a true friend?

What are the benefits of having a thankful friend?

How does John 15:14-15 support the concept that true friends are inclusive and not exclusive?

Why do you think so many friendships are exclusive and not inclusive?

List some ways you have seen friendships fall apart because they were exclusive?

Finding Support

Review and reflect.

Review the verse for the week and all five previous days of devotions.

What are the three biggest lessons you learned from this week's materials?

For each of those lessons, write a one-sentence statement explaining why it impressed you.

How does this material relate to staying pure and holy?

Day by Day

Day 6

CHAPTER 8   SETTING STANDARDS

It is often said that if you aim at nothing, you will certainly hit it. Most young people today have not even thought about standards let alone setting them. An important step in the road to purity and holiness is for you to set standards to which you will aspire. I Thessalonians 4:3-4 says, *"It is God's will that you should be holy, that you should avoid sexual immorality. That each of you should learn to control his own body in a way that is holy and honorable."*

Paul tells Timothy to *"Discipline yourself for the purpose of godliness."* (I Timothy 4:7a).

One definition of a *standard* is a flag that identifies an army or state. Another definition for standard is a rule set up or established by an authority. Both of these definitions apply to purity and holiness standards. The standards you live by should identify your allegiance to a kingdom...God's kingdom. They should also be principles that are founded on His authority, or guidelines that help you live out His call on your life.

Probably one of the greatest challenges ahead of you will be to be able to set standards with your head, commit to them with all your heart, and live by them even when your emotions are challenged. Setting standards of behavior means determining today what you will or will not do tomorrow. It means that you have thought about what is most important to you and you are committing to live out those values no matter what.

Often men have accepted the fallacy that setting standards for sexual purity in a relationship is a female responsibility. Too many good young men are not wrestling with these issues. Instead of setting their own standards and living by them, they accept the standards of the woman they are with and they try not to violate her wishes. A young man will be far more likely to keep standards if they are his own, adopted through his own understanding of the Word of God, and not standards that are put upon him by another human being, even if she is beautiful! So, let's look at areas in our lives where both young men and young women need to set personal standards.

Is God in first place?
Our need to know God should far outweigh the value of any human relationship we have now or will have in the future. It should be the overwhelming desire of each of us to know God on a deeper and more intimate level each day. For all of us,

the commitment to know God must supersede the need to enter a relationship with any other person. That very commitment will require that we set standards of behavior and of purity that are consistent with God's demands on our lives.

Guarding the input.

"I will set before my eyes no vile thing." (Psalm 101:3). *"I made a covenant with my eyes not to look lustfully at a girl."* (Job 31:1). In setting standards, you must evaluate the kind of materials you allow yourself to see. We are told that approximately 60% of the business transacted on the Internet is sexually related. Never before has pornography been more readily accessible in the private confines of our homes. Avoid it at all costs. Avoid even the nuances of pornography on certain television shows (You know which ones they are!) as well as the sexual lyrics of secular music; and simply do not allow yourself to go to see movies that are sexually explicit. There can be no exceptions! If you are serious about protecting your purity and holiness, you must first guard with persistence and determination all that enters through your eyes or ears.

Guarding the appearance.

Fashion is a concern for most of you today. The fear of not being accepted is real and the way you dress sometimes determines the degree to which you are accepted by your friends. The Bible instructs us not to been known or noted for our outward appearance. And the way we dress makes a definite statement about how we will be known. For Christians, modest, tasteful dress is a must. You don't have to look like you stepped out of your parents' generation, but you do have to make sure you are not dressing to call undue attention to yourself or to your body. God is far more concerned about you developing your inner man/woman and your inner beauty than He is about what you look like on the outside. If too much time, energy, and resources are spent on making the outside attractive, there will not be enough time, energy, and resources left for development of the heart. If you develop the inner qualities that God desires, you will be accepted by your friends for all the right reasons and not for reasons that may pull you away from a life of purity and holiness.

Guarding the heart.

Memorizing key portions of God's word can be a great deterrent to sin. The Bible tells us that hiding God's Word in our heart (memorizing scripture) keeps us from sinning against Him. Remember, when Christ was tempted in the wilderness by Satan, Jesus Himself responded by quoting God's Word. His example is one that we should follow.

Joshua 1:8 says that we should meditate on God's Word day and night. You can meditate on God's Word that constantly only if you have memorized portions of it. Memorization is a tool that will enable you to immerse yourself in the message of the Bible so that it is with you at all times. If you have verses stored in your memory,

"I made a covenant with my eyes not to look lustfully at a girl."   Job 31:1

the Holy Spirit can bring them to your attention when the message is most needed in your life. There is no substitute for having God's Word stored in your heart and mind.

So what scriptures should you memorize? I Thessalonians 4:3-8 is a powerful portion of God's Word that teaches us about purity and holiness. We recommend that you begin your memorization with that passage

From there, you may want to ask God to show you a verse that you can adopt as the theme verse for your life. Once He shows you this passage, memorize it, too, and keep it at the forefront of your mind at all times. It will serve as a continual reminder of God's leadership in your life and of your commitment to Him and His Word.

Bringing in reinforcements.

By now you may be wondering how your parents, guardians, or significant family members may be involved in your relationships. The general rule to follow is that the more they are involved, the better. Parental involvement is not a curse, but rather a great opportunity for you to enjoy godly relationships with a safety net in place to help, encourage, and protect. As we discussed in an earlier chapter, it may be time for you to approach your parents and tell them that you desire their involvement in your life especially in holding you accountable for purity and holiness standards that you set as we go through this chapter. Let them know what those standards are and keep open lines of communication with them. You and they will grow close in this process and you won't feel like you are out in a big world on your own. You will have reinforcements and support at the home base.

Defining love.

Many people are saying, "I love you", with only the faintest idea of what those words mean. We are constantly being told that people are seeking love, and yet they don't seem to even understand what it is that they are looking for. I Corinthians 13 gives us the greatest description of love that can be found anywhere. In the context of our discussion about memorizing God's Word, this chapter would be an excellent passage for you to commit to memory. You will never wonder again what real love, the ideal love, is like.

There are several types of love that are talked about in the New Testament. The first is identified by the Greek word *eros*. Eros is defined as sensual love and from it we derive our word *erotic*. The overriding characteristic of this type of love is that it focuses on sexual expression and gratification. Eros is a love for the physical body. We might best describe it as "Body Love".

A second type of love in scripture is identified by the Greek word *phileo* which means love for a brother. From this word, we derive the word *Philadelphia* which is known in the USA as the city of brotherly love. This kind of love is not as selfish as eros and is

Standards are roadblocks you put in the way to prevent you from going to areas of weakness in your life.

evidenced by friendship and by treating others as having importance. Phileo represents tender affection and a great humanitarian love that knows of its need to care for others. It can best be described as a "Head Love".

Finally, there is type of biblical love known as *agape*. This is the level of love Christ exercised when He gave himself up as a sacrifice for us. It is also the kind of love described in the I Corinthians 13 passage we just mentioned. Agape is characterized by a willingness to serve. It is unconditional caring and acceptance of another. It can best be described as a "Heart Love." It penetrates to the deepest recesses of our lives.

God loves us with agape love and it should be our goal, as seekers of godly relationships, to reserve our real love for the person that we feel we can love with God's great agape.

Being accountable.

We talked in the last chapter about establishing a relationship with an accountability partner or a mentor. This is just a reminder that you need to take the initiative and get that relationship in place. You can set standards, but those standards will be met only if we are willing to enter into true accountability with another person.

Choosing relationships.

What kind of person should you be looking for? With what kind of person can you establish the deep kind of personal commitment and agape love that we have described throughout this study? The answer "a Christian" is not acceptable. There's more to it than that! You should determine to seek only God's best, which means that you would not be satisfied with any less than being with a person who shares that goal and is growing in a committed relationship to God. We talked about evangelistic dating earlier – the idea of dating someone with the goal of winning them to Christ. If you are tempted to move in that direction, please review the instruction already given. There is nothing biblical about entering into a relationship with someone for this purpose.

Building relationships.

The most effective, most long-lasting way to build a solid relationship is to learn the value of good communication. Go where communication can be established! Too many relationships are being formed that never establish good communication and then when troubles come or when the rush of the initial excitement of the relationship fades, the couple finds that they have nothing left on which to build their future. Value and build communication now and that foundation will help you build a strong, life-long relationship.

It is important that you and your partner simply learn how to have fun together. Where can you go or who can you go with to enjoy laughter and good, clean, unadulterated fun? In order to find that

"Love is patient,

Love is kind ..."

I Corinthians 13

fun, you may have to plan your dates ahead of time and not just get together to figure something out. Even spontaneous moments have an element of plan and purpose ingrained. Think about what is fun for you and invite your date to join in. Then communicate about what is also fun for him or her and do what they like to do, too. Be creative. Enjoy the company of other young people – often the 'more the merrier' rule applies. There's always someone in a group who will naturally volunteer to be the life of the party. Nothing will endear you more to a person than the ability to have a good time together without going home with regrets.

In the interest of responsibility and accountability, make sure your parents know where you are going, who you will be with, what activities you have planned, and how late you plan to be. The road to trust is paved with concrete information.

Setting limits.
Before we get to the number one question we are asked by youth related to purity and holiness, answer this question, "Are you still cheating in school?" Yes or No? If you answer "yes" then you are a cheater. If you answer "no" then you were a cheater. It's called a dirty question because you can't walk away from it clean. One way or another you're incriminated.

If you ask the wrong question, you will always get the wrong answer. What students always want to know at this point in our study is how far they can go in their physical relationship with another person and still be considered by God to be pure and holy. That's a good example of the wrong question. Rather than asking how close you can get to sin, before it becomes sin you should be asking "How close can I get to God?"

The road to trust is paved with concrete information.

We suggest thinking on the following guidelines as you set your purity standards:

1. Any rule is poor if the attitude of the heart is wrong. Do you want to be pure?

2. Adhere to the Horizontal Rule. Two of us will not lie down together at any place or in any situation.

3. Refuse to be alone in any place that promotes physical intimacy. In other words, don't go to the other person's home when no one else is around.

4. Do only in private what you do in public even if adults were present.

5. If it is covered with clothing when the temperature is below 40 degrees, keep your hands off.

6. Do only what you would want your future spouse doing with someone.

7. If in doubt, don't do it.

8. Ask yourself if the proposed activity will lead to a growing respect and understanding of the other person.

9. Does this activity lead you to desiring more contact? If it does, step back.

10. Understand that relationships are progressive. Holding hands today becomes old hat tomorrow.

Planning a wholesome conclusion.

This is hard to do, but you and your partner need to agree ahead of time that there will be a predetermined line that, if crossed or attempted to be crossed, will bring the outing to an immediate end. That line is crossed if either of you engages in inappropriate actions, sexual conversation, or even subtle innuendoes. Think through the actions or words that, to you, would be cause an end to the event and then behave accordingly, asking that your partner to the same. God will honor your willingness to submit to His greater plan for your life.

How the outing will end is also important. As you work through this tough issue, please consider the following so you can plan for any eventuality:

- Who is available for a quick contact if you need back up or accountability support?
- What means do you have to make a quick contact with that person?
- What are safety factors that should be considered when planning the event?
- How would you inform the other person that the outing is over?
- What would be done if the other person refused to cooperate with your decision?

Committing to DRULL

Psalm 119:37a says, *"Turn my eyes away from worthless things…"*

Psalm 101:3a says, *"I will set before my eye no vile thing…"*

Job 31:1 says, *"I made a covenant with my eyes not to look lustfully at a girl."*

With these verses in mind, we recommend that standards include a commitment to what we call the DRULL Rule. What is the DRULL Rule? DRULL means that when you are placed in a position where lust has a chance to grow, instead of staying and looking (which can lead to more staying, looking, and lusting), you choose to look Down, Right, Up, Left and then Leave. If you do it quickly, the circular motion of the head helps create enough momentum to make

"I will set before my eye no vile thing…"

Psalm 101:3a

142

the first two steps of leaving easier.

Those of you who are football enthusiasts may be aware of a pass pattern known as the Down and Out. Down and Out is also an applicable rule when you are tempted in areas of lust. If you see a compromising event coming, don't wait. Look down and get out of there.

Format for setting standards.

How can you get started in the process of setting purity and holiness standards and surrounding yourself with support so that you can be able to meet those standards within your relationships? Many people begin with good intentions, but various obstacles stop the progress. We recommend six steps to setting standards.

1. Write your standards **now**.

    We encourage you to sit down and write out your purity standards within the next week while the thoughts are fresh in your mind and the desire to live a holy life is high. This is probably a good time in your life for setting these standards. Make the hard choices now, in the good days, so that when the compromising days stare you down, your decision has been made. It is easier to stay out of a bad situation than it is to get out of a bad situation.

2. Find an encourager.

    It may be a friend, mentor, youth pastor, or parent. Successful standard setting is enhanced when you find someone else who will encourage you, challenge you, and provide wise and honest feedback.

3. Set standards that matter to **you**.

    It is better to have a few standards specifically suited to your personality and needs, than to have an impressive list that you don't totally subscribe to. Ask yourself the question, "In the next year what are those areas where I will most be challenged?" Then write your standards to address those upcoming challenges.

4. Make standards accessible.

    Once standards are written, make copies that can be posted at places where you will be reminded of them. These are not posted for others to see, but rather, they are to be placed in locations where they serve as a reminder to you of your personal commitment.

Make the hard choices now, in the good days, so that when the compromising days stare you down, your decision has been made.

5. Share your standards with someone else.

The more you talk about the standards you have set and the more you share them with others, the more you will understand them and take them to heart. These standards become a part of you and who you identify yourself to be when you are talking to those who are close to you. The goal is that you will take real ownership the standards you have adopted.

6. Review standards periodically.

Good standards are always open to review. While some standards you set will be ongoing and steadfast, others will change as you mature. Excellent standard setting involves an ongoing process of review that allows for growth and deeper understanding emotionally, physically, and spiritually.

A Word of Caution.
Critics of standard setting state their fear of legalism and their caution that the standards could lead the way in your life rather than the Holy Spirit. Scripturally, we are told to go ahead and set our plans as long as we acknowledge the hand of the Lord in all we do. Proverbs 16:3 says, *"Commit to the Lord whatever you do, and your plans will succeed."*

So set your standards in an attitude of prayer and with the guidance of the Holy Spirit. You then will be following God's direction, doing so in a way that makes it easy for you to follow, and in a way that reminds you of the standards you and God together have set.

"Commit to the Lord whatever ou do and your plans will succeed."

Proverbs 16:3

Dig Deeper: Setting Standards

Three major recommendations, as you make your selection of a mentor and/or accountability partner, are as follows:

    1. Seek someone of the same sex as you are.

    2. Seek someone older than you are.

    3. Make a commitment to contact this person within one week of reading this chapter and discuss with him his willingness to be your mentor/accountability partner.

A mentor must be a person whose life you respect and someone after whom you would like to model your life to some degree. Is there anyone you can think of who will do more than help you stay pure and holy, but who would also be willing to help you grow in all areas of your walk with Jesus Christ? Make a list below of two or three individuals who would fit that role.

A mentor must be a person whose life you respect.

Journal Page

Take Action

Pray asking God to identify a statement and/or scripture that was meaningful to you in this chapter.

On your journal page, write this statement or scripture passage as well as any other thoughts or feelings you have in response to what you are learning.

Setting Standards

Memory Verse
"The heart of the discerning acquires knowledge; the ears of the wise seek it out" (Proverbs 18:15).

<u>**Special Note:**</u> I and II Timothy were written to Timothy by Paul who was training, discipling, and mentoring this younger man. It is full of wise words on life and godliness. A full reading of these two letters is recommended for those interested in seeking help.

Read II Timothy 2:20-22.

What does it mean to be "an instrument for noble purpose"?

Why do these verses say to "flee from the evil desires of youth"?

What did Paul tell Timothy to pursue?

Why do you think an older man like Paul told Timothy to flee rather than to stay and fight?

Outline a plan for fleeing and share it with a person of the same gender who is at least ten years older than you are.

Day by Day

Day 1

Setting Standards

Read I Timothy 4:11-14.

What is Paul's advice to Timothy in verse 12a?

List those things in the second half of verse 12 that Paul told Timothy to do.

Day by Day

Day 2

What other things was Paul encouraging Timothy to do?

What do you think a meeting between these two was like?

Who do you have encouraging you in this way? If there is no one doing that for you, then what will it take to find someone?

Setting Standards

Read Proverbs 12:15, 13:10, and 15:22.

According to Proverbs 15:22, why do plans fail?

In these verses, what is one of the differences between a fool and a wise man?

After reading Proverbs 13:20, state what pride breeds. What is a mark of wisdom?

Why are people fearful of sharing plans?

How does pride enter in to the picture in stopping the process of seeking help?

Describe a time in your life when seeking godly advice was helpful.

Day by Day

Day 3

Setting Standards

Read II Samuel 12:1-13.

Retell Nathan's story in summary form and in your own words.

How did David respond to this story?

Describe Nathan's confrontation of David.

How did David react to the confrontation?

Why is it hard to confront?

How and why would a person invite someone to be openly confrontational?

Setting Standards

Read Colossians 3:12-14.

Record all the things listed in this passage that we are commanded to put on.

Where could you find a person with these qualities?

How could you go about asking someone like this to help in a mentoring role?

What qualities would you ask such a person to help you develop?

What would hold you back from seeking someone out?

Day by Day

Day 5

Setting Standards

Review and reflect.

Review the verse for the week and all five previous days of devotions.

What are the three biggest lessons you learned from this week's materials?

For each of those lessons, write a one-sentence statement explaining why it impressed you.

How does this material relate to staying pure and holy?

Day by Day

Day 6

CHAPTER 9   MAKE A COMMITMENT

"He who rejects this instruction does not reject man, but God who gives you his Holy Spirit" (I Thessalonians 4:8).

Those are sobering words! Our prayer as you complete this study is that you have been both refreshed by and confronted with dynamic challenges from God's Word. However, all challenges are empty if you do not act on them. Thus, this final key to purity and holiness is putting into practice what you have learned! In a world where commitment often gives way to convenience, we are called to take a stand for Christ.

Joshua made a very bold commitment in Joshua 24:15, *"But suppose you don't want to serve him. Then choose for yourselves right now whom you will serve...But as for me and my family, we will serve the Lord."* In essence, Joshua had told Israel to commit to the Lord. He then followed it up with the challenge for them to make up their minds about whether or not they were going to follow his advice. As you conclude this study, we encourage you to commit to the Lord. In the same breath we remind you that the only way to make that commitment is to make up your mind to do so. Following God is an act of your will. You have to choose Him and His ways.

A young man approached me after a seminar several years ago, thanked me, and said he had enjoyed the time and had learned some things that he thought would help him, but he really didn't agree with the teaching. He planned to continue, in his words, "to fool around with girls until I meet the right one."

I inquired, "Do you understand what the Bible says about what you are doing?"

"Yes," he replied, "but I don't think it is that big of a deal."

I smiled, then asked a friend of his to come up next to us and to play the role of God in a short skit. The two of them looked at me curiously and then agreed to having him play this role.

I turned to 'God' and yelled as loud as I could, "Get out of my face, God! I want to do this one my way!"

They both laughed at the way I screamed at 'God' but also had on their faces a look which said, "You should never talk to God that way."

In our words we would never address God in such a way, but by our thoughts and attitudes we do exactly that. There is great solemnity in the words from I Thessalonians, *"...does not reject man, but God..."*

To have heard this material, to have comprehended parts of it, and even to have it make an emotional impact is good. The key issue in front of you now is how you are going to respond to the challenge you have been given. Let God and obedience to His Word bring about change in your life. I am fond of saying, "I'm sick and tired of people being moved, but not changed." An emotional experience can be great, but that does not mean it has any lasting impact. God is into life change! He wants you to be both moved and changed as you experience the deep joy of a life found only in relationship to Jesus and His ways.

As you make your decision regarding putting into practice this crucial issue of purity and holiness, please consider several factors.

Outward fanfare or inward condition.
Over the years I have witnessed hundreds of calls to commitment asking respondents to stand up, to kneel down, to walk forward, or to raise hands. As I am often the one who issues such calls, I can tell you from firsthand experience that I have seen some immediate and life-changing responses. At the same time I have seen some people in the audience with opened eyes checking out what others were doing so they could see what they thought would be the most appropriate thing to do. I have even seen other hands tugging and pulling someone into what the tugger and puller considered to be the proper response position.

A young man who had made a profession of faith in Christ during a week at a Christian camp showed no evidence of any change during a second week at camp. If anything, his conduct had worsened. I confronted him about his conduct and emphasized that, because he had accepted Christ the previous week, he should now desire to do things in love for others just as Jesus did. With outstretched finger pointed directly at his counselor, he boldly proclaimed, "He made me do it! He made me do it!" The outward response of commitment was not consistent with the inward heart which remained rebellious.

A commitment is not something that can be forced on you from the outside. We all try and desire to make others commit to things we feel will best serve their best interest (and many times ours also). But this is not about arm twisting or salesmanship. True commitment comes from within and is initiated by the Spirit of God. It is a determination and resolve rising from within you. You must be determined to pursue a certain path or decision. So, now, as you consider the call to purity and holiness, the overriding questions become, "What has God stirred within you? What response to the Holy Spirit's call do you need to make?"

A commitment is not some-thing that can be forced on you from the outside.

A commitment is not about being perfect. It is about being committed. Do not run away from commitment by fear of failure. We must remember that we are all sinners and have been saved by grace. The question here is one of intent. Is it your desire to walk in God's way and power in the area of purity and holiness? If your heart says 'yes', then it is time to take a stand. Will the battle go away? Will all struggles and temptations cease? The answer to these questions is 'no'. But the strength is in seeking and surrendering to the Lord. He then begins the process of purifying you and making you holy in His sight and in your actions.

One of the Ten Commandments reads, *"Do not misuse the name of the Lord your God. The Lord will find guilty anyone who misuses his name."* (Exodus 20:7). This command is usually quoted in connection with swearing or using vulgar language, but the concept goes far beyond those parameters. Anytime a person makes a commitment before God and does it simply to please others, to look good in front of the crowd, or to 'keep people off my back', that individual is misusing the Lord's name. If you make an outward commitment in the presence of God, but your heart is not in it, then your word is empty. It carries no meaning. The outward action and inward condition are in conflict. Take very seriously the commitments you make before the Lord. He does!

When does commitment begin?
The faces of 350 young women looked on as a trembling hand was raised. A sixteen-year-old, with tears in her eyes, blurted out the question that the others were afraid to ask. "Is it too late?" Recognizing her past sin and trying to understand God's love for her had brought her to a place of confusion. Can someone who already has sacrificed his or her physical purity make a commitment to be pure and holy, or is it simply too late?

Our God is a God who forgives, heals and restores. When the woman was caught in adultery (as recorded in John, chapter 8), the religious leaders were prepared to stone her. But when they brought her to Jesus, believing that He would condemn her, He stopped the proceedings. He bent down and began to write in the dirt. Many suggest that he was writing the names of women who were 'acquaintances' of the men getting ready to do the stoning. Others suggest he was writing down the secret sins of those standing nearby. Whatever He wrote, reading the writings caused the crowd to disperse rather quickly.

As the condemned woman looked up into the eyes of Jesus, He said two things to her both of which are of great significance. First, He asked, *"Woman, where are they? Has no one condemned you?"* (John 8:10). They were gone, and the only one who remained was Jesus. Guess what? He was perfect! He was the only one who had the right to condemn her, but He did not. The very one who could have hurled the first, second, and third stones stood there and did not put

Is

it

too

late?

her down, but rather He lifted her up.

His next words give us great insight into a commitment to living a life of purity. *"Then neither do I condemn you. . . Go now and leave your life of sin"* (John 8:11). His statement recognized that she was a sinner; her actions had been impure and wrong, but He told her to go. He didn't instruct her to hide in shame for the rest of her life, but rather to be out and doing. But while she was out there, she was to live a changed life. She was to abandon her past and "sin no more." Jesus' treatment of this desperate, defeated woman is a perfect example of God's forgiving, healing and restoration.

In another instance, recorded in John 4, Christ confronted a woman at a well in Samaria. She told Him that she had no husband. Jesus revealed that He knew there had been many men in her life with whom she lived but to whom she had not been married. Again, instead of condemning her, Jesus confronted the sin, extended forgiveness, and sent her on her way. When she returned to her town, she was excited and cried out, *"Come, see a man who told me everything I ever did."* (John 4:29). Do you catch the significance of her statement? In essence she is saying, "I met Someone who knows everything about me, and He still forgave me and sent me on my way in love."

Finally, so the picture painted doesn't simply reflect only on women, we can examine the life of David. His adulterous affair with Bathsheba not only resulted in an unplanned pregnancy but also in David's murder of Bathsheba's husband, Uriah. Once confronted with his sin, David cried out to God by saying, *"Create in me a pure heart, O God..."* (Psalm 51:10). God honored his repentance and his changed life and now David stands in the lineage of Jesus and is called *"a man after God's own heart"* (I Samuel 13:14).

Do you see the pattern in the Bible? Regardless of where you have been, God desires that your life be surrendered to Him today. He will restore you to relationship with Him and will create in you a pure heart just as He did for David. God is more concerned about where you are going than where you have been.

> If your life has been lived in purity and holiness, then today serves as a day to reaffirm the commitment you made previously.

> If such a commitment has never been made, the challenge in front of you at this moment is to accept the purity and holiness standards from this day forward.

> If past sin clouds your life, then today is the day to seek forgiveness, healing, and restoration and begin the journey from this day forward.

"Create in me a pure heart, O God"

Psalm 51:10

The good news is that the answer to the question, "Is it too late?" is a resounding "No!"

I John 1:9 says, *"If we confess our sins he is faithful and just to forgive us our sins and purify us from all unrighteousness."*

In the announcement by angels of Jesus' birth, the purpose of His coming was stated, *"…you are to give him the name Jesus, because he will save his people from their sins"* (Matthew 1:21).

Psalm 103:12 says, *"As far as the east is from the west, so far has he removed our transgressions from us."*

The stated purpose in Jesus' coming was to save us and cleanse us from our sins. You can take Him up on that promise, accept the payment He made for your sinfulness, and, with the fallen woman of John 8, *"Go now and leave your life of sin"* (John 8:11). He came for the express purpose of forgiving, restoring, and healing. Let Him do it for you.

In summary, if you come today as one who has walked in godliness in your relationships, then praise God and commit to make it a desire of your life to continue in the path you have chosen. If you have come to this study as one who has already made such a commitment, then reaffirm it today, and move forward in boldness for Christ. Finally, if you are one who has not walked in godliness, then seek forgiveness and cleansing then move ahead in your commitment from this day forward.

A word regarding innocence.
Without a doubt, there are those studying this material who, sadly, have been the victims of sexual abuse. This behavior can carry scars that make you feel impure and even unholy. For these victims, we offer the comfort of Jesus' teaching in Mark 7:14-23.

> *"Again Jesus called the crowd to him and said, "Listen to me, everyone and understand this. Nothing outside a man can make him unclean by going into him. Rather, it is what comes out of a man that makes him unclean. After he had left the crowd entered the house, his disciples asked him about this parable. Are you so dull? He asked. Don't you see that nothing that enters a man from the outside can make him unclean? For it doesn't go into his heart but his stomach and then out of his body… He went on, What comes out of a man is what makes him unclean. For from within, out of men's hearts, come evil thoughts, sexual immorality, theft, murder, adultery, greed, malice, deceit, lewdness, envy, slander, arrogance, and folly. All these evils come from inside and make a man unclean."*

Some will be quick to point out that the parable starts over a

I believe in a God who heals, forgives and restores.

conversation about eating the right things. But as the passage comes to an end, a long list of sins emerge that have nothing to do with food and eating habits.

If anyone has been sexually abused, he or she is not impure or unholy as a result. The victim is not the sinner. Sin comes from the heart. A sinful act performed by someone else, does not make the victim impure. There is great comfort and healing within these verses for those who have been victimized. If you have been the victim of sexual abuse, please do not hesitate to seek out wise Christian counsel for help in overcoming the emotional scars that result from such actions. There are those who are able to help. You might ask your youth pastor or pastor for suggestions as to whom you can call.

Visible reminders.
Why should someone make an outward gesture in the form of signing a card, filling in a workbook, going forward in a meeting, or whatever else may be suggested as a sign of genuine commitment? Once again, the Bible gives us teaching about the need for us as humans to have reminders of significant turning points in our lives and reminders of spiritual commitments that we make.

After all the people had successfully crossed the Jordan River, God instructed Joshua, in Joshua chapter 4, to send back one representative from each of the twelve tribes to pick up a stone from the middle of the riverbed. They then laid those stones at the place where the children of Israel stayed the first night on the other side of the Jordan. When the Israelites asked why they were doing this, Joshua responded, *"When your children ask you, 'What do these stones mean?' Then tell them that the flow of the Jordan was cut off before the ark of the covenant of the Lord…These stones are to be a memorial to the people of Israel forever"* (Joshua 4:6-7).

The Lord's Supper was also given to us as a feast of remembrance. The bread and juice serve as a reminder of what Christ accomplished for us on the cross. *"For whenever you eat this bread and drink this cup, you proclaim the Lord's death until he comes."* (I Corinthians 11:26). The Lord's Supper is not a morbid event but rather one of great celebration. It is good to revisit our decision to accept Christ as our Savior and remember that it was through His death on the cross that we are made new. The Lord has determined and instructed that is good to set in place events or objects that will help us remember commitments and events.

One past participant shared that as a wedding gift for her new husband, she gave him the purity and holiness commitment card she had signed years earlier. She had attached a note to that card which said, "Just for you!" To some that may sound sappy or old fashioned, but to the man who received it, it was a very special gift. Others have shared about taking out their commitment card early in a new relationship and sharing their commitment with their partner

A sinful act, performed by someone else does not make the victim impure.

158

as a means of opening up dialog. The act of signing or having the card is not the issue, but the card itself can be used as a great tool for remembering, sharing and revisiting your commitment during tough days.

The Bible record tells of many tough days for the children of Israel after they crossed the Jordan River. During those times, it was good for them to revisit that spot of triumph and joy and reflect on what God had done for them there and of what He had promised to do for them in the Promised Land. We wholeheartedly recommend that first you make a commitment to purity and holiness and that you then set up an object of remembrance.

Today, we often call a time of commitment as a defining moment. A defining moment is simply a time when a decision is made that impacts the rest of your life. Do you have to have some physical sign of commitment such as signing the card you will find later in this book? God knows your heart and the real issue is the commitment that you make there. But why would you not be willing to show some kind of outward evidence of your internal commitment? In a world that prefers to have us Christians sit down and shut up about purity and holiness, it is time we stand up and speak up. The Bible says, *"Whoever acknowledges me before men, I will also acknowledge him before my Father in heaven. But whoever disowns me before men, I will disown him before my Father in heaven"* (Matthew 10:32-33).

The strength of sharing.
The car motor stalls. The young man looks across the seat, shrugs his shoulders and pats the seat next to him. "Why don't you slide over and sit next to me, Sweetheart?" comes to her in his still changing voice. She slides over, only to have his arm move in gyrations as he stretches and ultimately slips it around her shoulder. Next, he moves into the snuggle mode, slowly grinding his head into her soft shoulder.

At this point, she springs into action and shouts, "Let me show you a card with a life commitment on it!" She proudly displays a purity and holiness card signed by herself and her accountability partner. The words from I Thessalonians 4:3-8 stare him in the face as it says, *"It is God's will that you should be holy. That you should avoid sexual immorality, that each of you should learn to control your own body in a way that is holy and honorable…"* She looks at him and says, "See, I made that commitment and if your intent is to challenge it, you might as well start this vehicle and take me home now."

As you share your commitment with others, it gains strength. Talking to people about this step will reinforce your decision to commit. Often people have shared that others, after hearing their stories, have commented about the respect they have gained, or how their life would have been better had they made such a commitment at an early stage. You will be surprised at what a good discussion starter this

A defining moment is simply a time when a decision is made that impacts the rest of your life.

kind of honest and heartfelt sharing can be.

For many, the first stand is the toughest. To show someone the card, to share the concept of your commitment, or to openly share what God has done in your life can be frightening. However, I am amazed at how many times the response to sharing is so positive that the sharer is encouraged to do so again and again. Of course, not all people will agree and some will even mock your commitment, but the major point remains, and that is that strength comes from sharing about what you have committed. It is our goal that you will be so enthused about your purity and holiness decision that you will seek out opportunities to share your testimony with others.

Finally, you should know that your willingness to share your commitment may be the single factor prompting someone else to make a similar decision. After years of experience, I am convinced that there are many individuals who sense the need to make such a commitment, but they need to find someone who has been there, who has already made the decision, and for whom it is making a difference. As you take your stand, you very likely will experience the joy of finding others who desire to stand with you. You can be just the change agent they need in their lives!

Now is best.
The world is full of people who are ready to begin something tomorrow. The problem is that tomorrow never comes. II Corinthians 6:2b says, *"I tell you, now is the time of* God's *favor, now is the day of salvation."* When is the best time to make a commitment to living life God's way? The answer is **now**! Some people say they will make such a decision once they get a few things in order. If you wait until everything is in order, you will never make a commitment.

The alarm clock goes off at 5:45 am. You roll over and praise God for the snooze button. Ah yes, nine more minutes. Then you remember that this was the day that morning exercise was to become part of your daily regimen. You get up, look outside, and notice a few wet spots on the sidewalk and rationalize that it is too wet to walk this morning. You crawl back under the covers, turn off the alarm, and praise God for the gentle rain. Yes, I have been there too.

Too often we are waiting for the difficult times to force us to make decisions. Instead, we need to learn to make the hard decisions during the good times. If you wait to make a purity commitment at a time when the temptation to immorality is staring you in the face and your hormones have kicked in to high gear, you will fail. Now is the best time, when you have just focused on learning about God's plan for relationships, to make that tough decision. At this time you are also more apt to pursue finding the accountability person who will stand with you in those trying moments.

"I tell you, now is the time of God's favor, now is the day of salvation."

II Corinthians 6:26

160

Remember, *"He who rejects this instruction does not reject man but God who gives you his Holy Spirit"* (I Thessalonians 4:8).

As you think about the commitment to purity and holiness, we want to remind you from God's Word to set standards that help you to...

> ... be holy.
> ... avoid sexual immorality.
> ... control your own body in a way that is holy
>   and honorable.
> ... not act in passionate lust like the heathen.
> ... know God.
> ... not wrong your brother/sister or take advantage
>   of him/her.
> ... not be impure, but to live a holy life.
> ... keep this instruction and not reject God who
>   gives you His Holy Spirit.
> ... act in brotherly love.

Begin by reviewing your workbook, particularly the points you felt the Lord called to your attention in your journaling times and prayerfully considering the list we have given under Knowing God below. Then, on the following page, write out your own standards asking God to guide your thinking and your commitment.

Knowing God.

As you set your standards for purity and holiness, think about these ways in which your standards can be consistent with the Word of God and with knowing God on a closer and closer basis as you grow in Him and in obedience to Him.

> • Controlling what will you look at:
>   Internet, magazines, TV, or movies
> • Monitoring your physical appearance
> • Memorizing I Thessalonians 4:3-8
> • Enlisting parental involvement
> • Memorizing 1 Timothy 5:1-2
> • Learning a true definition of love
> • Being accountable to mature believer
> • Setting limits on how far you will go physically
>   in a relationship
> • Limiting where you will go
> • Determining the kinds of people with whom you
>   will spend your time
> • Adopting a theme verse
> • Committing to DRULL Rule and Down and Out

"He who rejects this instruction does not reject man, but God who gives you his Holy Spirit.

I Thessalonians 4:8

Take Action

Pray asking God to identify a statement and/or scripture that was meaningful to you in this chapter.

On your journal page, write this statement or scripture passage as well as any other thoughts or feelings you have in response to what you are learning.

Making a Commitment

Memory Verse: *"Finally, brothers, goodbye. Aim for perfection, listen to my appeal, be of one mind, live in peace. And the God of love and peace will be with you"* (II Corinthians 13:11).

Read Proverbs 16:3 and 9 and Proverbs 3:5-6 and 21-22.

Prayer should precede plans. Based on Proverbs 16:3 and 9, do you agree or disagree? Why or why not?

Why is it good to set standards before you begin in dating relationships?

As you set standards, how do you use Proverbs 3:5-6?

Explain Proverbs 3:21-22 in view of setting standards.

List as many good reasons as you can think of for setting purity and holiness standards.

Day by Day

Day 1

163

Making a Commitment

Read Romans 12:1-2, Exodus 12:5, Leviticus 22:21, and I Peter 1:18-19.

According to these verses, how does God see us?

Day by Day

Day 2

What were the requirements for a sacrifice in the Old Testament?

According to I Peter 1:18-19, how does Christ fit as a sacrifice?

Keeping these thoughts in mind, how should we view standards?

List some possible areas where you should consider setting standards.

Making a Commitment

Read Psalm 101:3, Job 31:1, and II Samuel 11:2-4.

What do these two biblical writers say about their eyes?

What are some ways through which things come before our eyes today?

What are some practical ways by which you could control what you see?

In the II Samuel reference, David saw Bathsheba. At what point did he sin?

Sight not only leads us to sin, but what we hear and say can be sinful in itself. Discuss how our senses are used to lure us to sin today.

Day by Day

Day 3

Making a Commitment

Read Philippians 2:3 and Matthew 22:37-40.

When setting standards, how should I view others?

Day by Day

Day 4

Describe what "selfish ambition" or "vain conceit" might look like.

What effect should these verses have on your set of standards?

What are some areas in which you tend to be selfish?

How will selfishness affect relationships?

Making a Commitment

Read I Corinthians 15:58, 16:13 and James 4:7.

Rewrite either I Corinthians 15:58 or 16:13 in your own words.

How can you learn to stand firm in today's world?

What is the verse in James instructing us to do?

Most people do not want to write standards. Why not?

In order to stand firm in your faith, how will setting standards be an asset?

Day by Day

Day 5

Write below your anticipated starting and completion dates for writing of your standards.

Making a Commitment

Review and reflect.

Review the verse for the week and all five previous days of devotions.

What are the three biggest lessons you learned from this week's materials?

Day by Day

Day 6

For each of those lessons, write a one-sentence statement explaining why it impressed you.

How does this material relate to staying pure and holy?

"It is God's will that you should be sanctified; that you should avoid sexual immorality; that each of you should learn to control his own body in a way that is holy and honorable, not in passionate lust like the heathen, who do not know God; and that in this matter no one should wrong his brother or take advantage of him. The Lord will punish men for all such sins, as we have already told you and warned you. For God did not call us to be impure, but to live a holy life. Therefore, he who rejects this instruction does not reject man but God, who gives you his Holy Spirit" (I Thessalonians 4:3-8).

I, _____, on

_____ do hereby from this day forward commit myself to living a life of purity and holiness.

I also give permission for the witness below to hold me accountable for my actions that may affect my staying pure and holy.

_____
Signature   Date

_____
Witness Signature   Date

Making

a

Commitment

to Purity

&

Holiness

Dig Deeper: Making a Commitment

As you prepare to set your three personal goals, ask yourself these questions:

- Am I DOING THINGS that will help me be pure and holy?
- Am I GOING PLACES that will help me be pure and holy?
- Am I seeking a PARTNER who will help me be pure and holy?
- Am I SETTING STANDARDS that will help me be pure and holy?
- Am I WITH FRIENDS who will help me be pure and holy?
- Am I SETTING MYSELF UP FOR SUCCESS or failure by the
    way I'm living?

The journey to purity is ongoing. Setting goals today will help you tomorrow. Also be aware that you have an enemy who would wish to snatch from you what has happened in this study.

I am setting the following three goals for myself in my quest to remain pure and holy from this day forward.

1.

2.

3.

For Goal #1, I will

For Goal #2, I will

For Goal #3, I will

The journey to purity is ongoing.

Making a Commitment

Memory Verse: "*When you make a vow to God, do not delay in fulfilling it. He has no pleasure in fools; fulfill your vow*" (Ecclesiastes 5:4).

Read Matthew 5:33-37.

What is an oath?

List the things we are told not to swear by and why?

From verse 37, describe how God desires our words to be.

How does God view our commitments?

How does this concept relate to purity and holiness?

Day by Day

Day 1

Making a Commitment

Read I Corinthians 9:24-27 and Philippians 3:12-14.

How does one "run to receive the prize"?

Day by Day

Day 2

What are some examples of strict training that an athlete endures?

What are some examples of strict training that a person committed to purity and holiness could go through?

Describe what Paul did to make sure he ran the race properly? Do you think he ever wanted to quit? (see II Corinthians 4:7-12)

Describe where you are in your race to be pure and holy.

Making a Commitment

Read Ecclesiastes 5:4-7, Proverbs 13:3, and II Timothy 4:7-8.

What is your first reaction as you read these verses?

Put Ecclesiastes 5:4-7 in your own words.

How can your mouth lead you into sin?

What does it mean to stand in awe of God?

How do these verses relate to purity and holiness?

Day by Day

Day 3

Making a Commitment

Read Proverbs 8:17, Luke 11:9, I Corinthians 10:13, James 1:25 and 4:7, and Isaiah 66:2.

God keeps His Word. . .

. . .to the seeker: What is the promise God gives to the seeker in Proverbs 8:17 and Luke 11:9?

. . .to the tempted: What is the promise God gives in I Corinthians 10:13?

. . .to the obedient: What is the promise in James 1:25 that is given to those who are obedient?

. . .to the humble: What is the promise given to the humble in Isaiah 66:2?

Day by Day

Day 4

Making a Commitment

Read

Insert first question.

What do these verses say about the way we should seek after God's command to be pure and holy?

What are some reasons people do not pursue God's commands with all of their heart?

From Deuteronomy 6, what are the instructions given regarding God's command?

Briefly describe the key elements needed in keeping your commitments.

Day by Day

Day 5

Making a Commitment

Review and reflect.

Review the verse for the week and all five previous days of devotions.

What are the three biggest lessons you learned from this week's materials?

For each of those lessons, write a one-sentence statement explaining why it impressed you.

How does this material relate to staying pure and holy?